THE LITTLE GUID

COOKIES

THE LITTLE GUIDES

COOKIES

FOG CITY PRESS

Published by Fog City Press
814 Montgomery Street
San Francisco, CA 94133 USA
Reprinted in 2000 (three times), 2001

Chief Executive Officer: John Owen
President: Terry Newell
Publisher: Sheena Coupe
Associate Publisher: Lynn Humphries
Art Director: Sue Burk
Managing Editor: Helen Bateman
Senior Designer: Kylie Mulquin
Editorial Coordinators: Sarah Anderson, Tracey Gibson
Production Manager: Helen Creeke
Production Coordinator: Kylie Lawson
Business Manager: Emily Jahn
Vice President International Sales: Stuart Laurence

Project Editor: Susan Tomnay
Designer: Jacqueline Richards

A catalog record for this book is available from
the Library of Congress, Washington, DC.

ISBN 1 875137 62 9

Color reproduction by Colourscan Co Pte Ltd
Printed by Leefung Asco Printers
Printed in China

A Weldon Owen Production

CONTENTS

PART TWO
KINDS OF COOKIES

Introduction

It is hard — no, it's almost impossible — to keep a cookie jar filled. No matter how many batches of vanilla-scented sugar cookies, craggy chocolate-dotted drop cookies, or elegant meringue kisses come out of the oven, they seem to disappear almost before they cool. And it isn't only little hands that reach for these delectable treats. Everyone succumbs to their fragrant allure.

In this collection of recipes you will find many that will evoke sweet memories of childhood favorites lovingly prepared in a kitchen perfumed with the warm smells of spices. Others will be entirely new, created to appeal to more sophisticated, grown-up tastes. All reflect years of combined culinary experience that ensures a successful result every time you bake.

Like each volume in the *Little Guides* series, the recipes are presented in a vivid step-by-step format designed for cooks of all skill levels. Every important stage of cookie making, from measuring to mixing to shaping, plus all the professional tricks for decorating and finishing, is included. Each is explained in easy-to-understand language and presented in full-color photographs. It's all there at a glance, as if you were back in your grandmother's kitchen or looking over the shoulder of a friendly expert baker.

An introductory chapter covers the basics, including how to store finished cookies properly to maintain their just-baked freshness. Succeeding chapters highlight a particular type of cookie, including all the favorites: drop cookies; bars; whimsical cutouts; sliced, shaped, and molded cookies; pressed spritz; and specialities such as French madeleines and Italian biscotti. Every chapter is color-coded and each recipe features a "steps-at-a-glance" box that uses these colors for quick reference to the photographic steps necessary for its

preparation. Tips appear virtually on every page, from basic equipment needs to helpful hints to a glossary of ingredients. And there are pages here and there devoted to special ingredients.

Consider this book your personal recipe file. Don't hesitate to make notes, if you need to, when variations come to mind. The recipes are so inventive and the directions so clearly explained that you just might create something new as you go along.

U.S. cup measures are used throughout this book. Slight adjustments may need to be made to quantities if Imperial or Metric cups are used.

9

PART ONE

THE BASICS

Here you'll find all you need to know about making cookies, with step-by-step instructions for measuring, mixing, icing and storing. There's also a guide to the equipment you'll need for better baking.

Making Cookie Dough

No other kind of baking is as simple and informal as making cookies. Whether you are a long-time cookie baker or a novice enthusiast, you will find inspiration in the pages that follow. The basic techniques demonstrated in this chapter will give you the skills to keep your cookie jar filled with the sweet, irresistible confections that appear in every chapter of this book.

Success also depends on using the right equipment. For best results, use baking sheets made from shiny, heavyweight aluminum with low sides or with a lip on one edge. Baking pans with high, straight sides will block heat and cause cookies to bake unevenly, while insulated sheets heat so slowly that cookies may require a different baking time than specified in these recipes. Also avoid dark sheets, as they absorb heat and may cause overbrowning. While the best procedure is to bake on the center rack of your oven, you can bake two sheets on different levels at one time and switch positions halfway through baking.

BASIC TOOLS FOR MAKING COOKIE DOUGH

If you bake at all, you probably have the equipment you'll need for making cookie dough: an electric mixer and bowl, measuring cups or accurate scales, spatulas, knives, a cutting board and spoons.

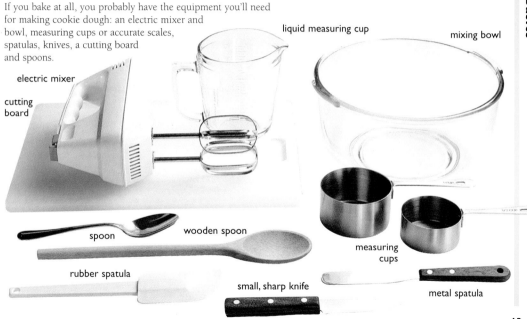

liquid measuring cup

mixing bowl

electric mixer

cutting board

spoon

wooden spoon

measuring cups

rubber spatula

small, sharp knife

metal spatula

scoop the flour into accurate scales for the most precise measurement

STEP 1

Measuring Flour

Before spooning the flour into the measuring cup or scales, stir it lightly with a fork in the canister to lighten it. Then fill the cup or scales with flour, but don't pack it down. Level the cup measure by sweeping across the top with a small metal spatula or a knife.

when measuring granulated sugar, spoon it into a dry measuring cup, then level off with a spatula

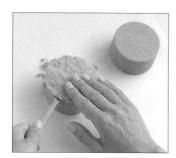

STEP 2

Measuring Brown Sugar

Spoon brown sugar into the measuring cup so that it rises in a mound slightly above the rim. Press the brown sugar firmly into the cup with your hand. To unmold, turn upside down and tap lightly; the sugar will hold the shape of the cup.

rinse the measuring cup with boiling water before adding the shortening to make it easier to remove

STEP 3

Measuring Shortening

Fill a measuring cup with shortening. Press the shortening firmly into the cup with a rubber spatula. Level off by sweeping across the rim with the spatula or a knife.

don't use margarine when a recipe, such as shortbread, specifically calls for butter

STEP 4

Measuring Butter or Margarine

Don't have the butter or margarine too soft or it won't cut cleanly and accurately. With a sharp knife, cut through the butter or margarine following the measurement guidelines printed on the paper. Let it soften fully before making dough.

STEPS FOR MAKING COOKIE DOUGH

set the cup flat on the counter so the surface of the liquid aligns with the markings

sticky liquids like honey will pour out smoothly if the measuring cup is first brushed lightly with oil

STEP 5

Measuring Liquids

Set a glass or plastic liquid measuring cup on a work surface. Add the liquid. For greatest accuracy, check the measurement at eye level rather than from above.

scrape the sides of the bowl once or twice with a rubber spatula

STEP 6

Mixing Dough

Using an electric mixer, prepare the dough according to the recipe directions up to the point of adding the flour. The dough will still stir easily and won't strain the motor of the mixer.

some portable mixers do not have motors that are powerful enough to incorporate all of the flour

STEP 7

Stirring in Remaining Flour
Beat in as much flour as you can using the electric mixer (the dough will become stiff). Stir in any remaining flour by hand with a wooden spoon until the dough is a homogeneous mixture with no streaks of flour showing.

Homemade cookies make wonderful and much-appreciated gifts. These are Fruity Foldovers (page 172), wrapped in tissue paper and packaged in a pretty box. Pack them just before you plan to give them, so they don't become soggy, and give them a final sprinkling with confectioners sugar before you put them into the box. Another way to package cookies for gift-giving is to gently place them in a glass jar and tie up with ribbon, or wrap in cellophane and secure with ribbon or colored raffia.

BASIC TOOLS FOR MAKING TOPPINGS AND MERINGUE

Essential equipment for preparing toppings and
meringue includes an electric mixer and mixing bowls,
spoons for measuring and stirring, a baking pan, wire
rack, fine-meshed sieve, and a small saucepan for
melting chocolate.

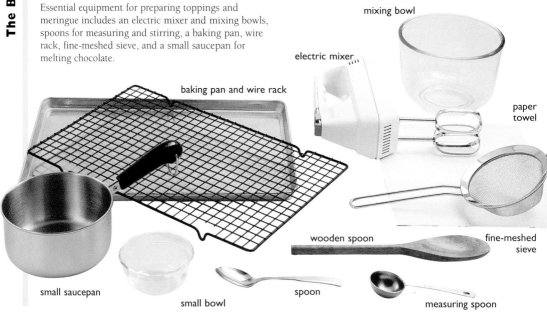

mixing bowl

electric mixer

paper
towel

baking pan and wire rack

fine-meshed
sieve

wooden spoon

small saucepan

small bowl

spoon

measuring spoon

Making Toppings and Meringue

Chocolate, sugar, eggs, nuts: these ingredients turn up again and again in every type of cookie, whether dropped from a spoon, baked in a pan, piped from a pastry bag, or formed with a cutter. The steps on these pages explain how to achieve a few of the more common uses for these popular additions. Not only will you come across these techniques in recipes throughout the book, you'll also find them used in almost all types of baking, so they are good tricks to know. You will learn how to melt chocolate to flavor dough or to decorate it, to make that miraculous cloudlike product of egg white and sugar called meringue, to toast nuts so they are aromatic and rich, and to remove their skins the easy way. You'll see how to apply icing in a network of fine lines, a technique known as drizzling, and how to pipe icing or melted chocolate from a heavy-duty plastic bag instead of using a piping bag with nozzle.

the chocolate will melt more quickly if first broken into small pieces; stirring over low heat prevents the chocolate on the bottom of the pan from scorching

STEP 1

Melting Chocolate

Place chocolate pieces and shortening (if required) in a small, heavy saucepan. Cook over low heat, stirring often, until melted and smooth. Or, place in a glass dish and microwave on high power for 1 to 3 minutes, or melt in a heavy-duty plastic bag as shown on page 39.

toasting nuts enhances their flavor and deepens their color

STEP 2

Toasting Nuts

Preheat an oven to 350°F/180°C/Gas Mark 4. Spread the nut halves or pieces in a single layer in a baking sheet. Bake until the nuts have colored slightly to a light golden brown, about 5 to 10 minutes. Stir once or twice with a wooden spoon so the nuts brown evenly.

nuts used for topping look better
without this papery skin; this step isn't
necessary for nuts stirred into a batter

STEP 3

Sifting Nuts

After the nuts have been toasted
and chopped (if required), spoon
them into a fine wire-mesh sieve set
over paper towelling. Tap the edge
of the sifter to filter out the skin.

*Chopped nuts make an
ideal topping for all kinds
of cookies. Here they're
sprinkled on Hazelnut Toffee
Bars (page 96), but they're just
as good on any kind of hearty
cookie. It's best to use more delicate
toppings for dainty cookies. Be careful
of giving nut-topped cookies to very
small children, especially if the nuts are
coarsely chopped. They can become lodged in
a young child's throat and may cause choking.
Sprinkles or nonpareils are a safer substitute.*

21

you can also
drizzle icing or
chocolate with
a fork

STEP 4

Drizzling Icing or Chocolate

Arrange cooled cookies on a wire rack over waxed paper.
Fill a small spoon with icing or melted chocolate. Move
the spoon back and forth over each cookie to create fine
lines. Let the icing or chocolate flow off the spoon in a
ribbon. Leave to set.

For a more
regular pattern,
use a piping bag
and small round
nozzle

STEP 5

Piping Icing or Chocolate

This is a quick way to pipe icing or melted chocolate
without the use of a piping bag and nozzle. Spoon icing
or melted chocolate into a heavy-duty plastic bag, and
cut a tiny piece off one corner. Squeeze the bag gently to
pipe the chocolate in a thin drizzle.

STEPS FOR MAKING MERINGUE

STEP 1

Adding Sugar

With an electric mixer on medium speed, beat the egg whites until they are white and foamy and the tips of the peaks bend over when the beaters are lifted out (soft peaks). Gradually add sugar, 1 tablespoon at a time.

STEP 2

Beating to Stiff Peaks

Continue beating the egg whites and sugar until the mixture begins to stiffen. The meringue is ready when it looks glossy and forms stiff peaks when the beaters are lifted out.

Storing Cookies

Although it is a rare batch that lasts more than a few days without being devoured down to the very last crumb, cookies can go stale quickly unless protected against air or excess moisture. Proper storage also prevents them from breakage or other damage.

Let cookies cool completely on a wire rack, then arrange in an airtight container as shown in the step on page 27. They will keep at room temperature for up to 3 days. If you prefer, leave bar cookies in their baking tin, tightly covered with plastic wrap or aluminum foil. Store soft and crisp cookies separately, or the crisp ones will absorb moisture from the others and become soft themselves. On the other hand, you can revive soft cookies that have dried out and hardened by placing a wedge of apple or a slice of bread on a piece of waxed paper and placing it on top of the cookies in the closed container. Remove after 1 day.

For longer storage, freeze uniced cookies in heavy-duty freezer bags or freezer containers. They will stay fresh for up to 1 year. When needed, let them thaw completely before you decorate.

BASIC TOOLS FOR STORING COOKIES

To keep cookies fresh, store them
in airtight containers between
layers of waxed paper.

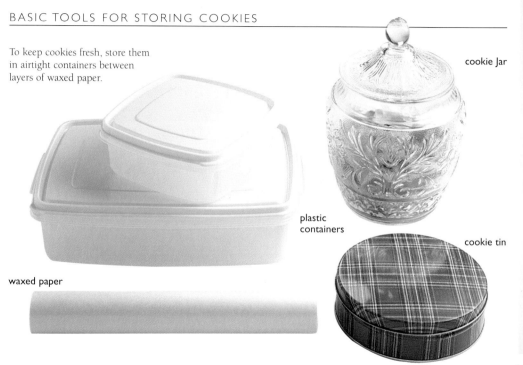

cookie Jar

plastic
containers

cookie tin

waxed paper

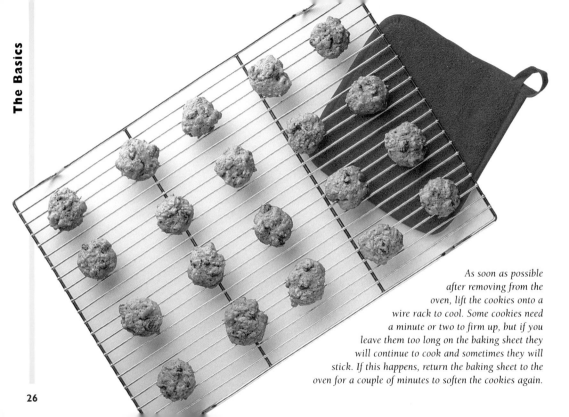

As soon as possible after removing from the oven, lift the cookies onto a wire rack to cool. Some cookies need a minute or two to firm up, but if you leave them too long on the baking sheet they will continue to cook and sometimes they will stick. If this happens, return the baking sheet to the oven for a couple of minutes to soften the cookies again.

waxed paper keeps each layer of cookies free of crumbs

STEP 1

Storing Cookies

Select a storage container that allows easy access to the cookies inside. Arrange the cookies in layers in the container. If the cookies are soft, place a sheet of waxed paper between each layer. Seal the container airtight.

PART TWO

KINDS OF COOKIES

Cookies can be dropped from a spoon, cut into bars or shapes,
sliced, molded, pressed, or even made into a little cottage.
And the variety of shapes, flavors and decorations
you can use is practically
unlimited.

DROP COOKIES

BASIC TOOLS FOR MAKING DROP COOKIES

Use a large bowl and wooden spoon for drop cookie dough, plus smaller bowls for additions like nuts or dried fruit. A pair of tablespoons or teaspoons is all you need to transfer the dough to the baking sheet. Transfer cookies to a cooling rack with a wide metal spatula.

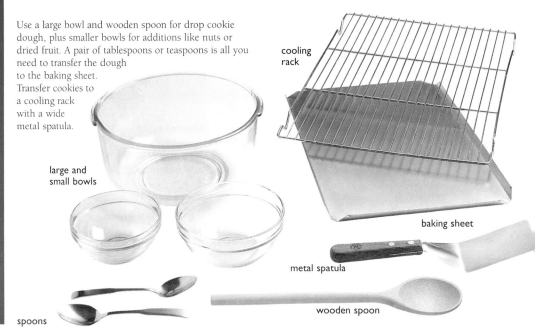

cooling rack

large and small bowls

baking sheet

metal spatula

spoons

wooden spoon

Making Drop Cookies

Making drop cookies is a simple craft. No artistry is required, only a gentle push to transfer the dough from spoon to baking sheet. As they bake, the soft, chunky mounds spread and settle into charmingly irregular rounds with homely appeal that are perfect with a good cup of coffee or a frosty glass of milk.

Not only are drop cookies easy to prepare, but they have a wonderful versatility. By varying a few ingredients or adjusting the proportions, you can change this kind of cookie dramatically. Their texture can be chewy, like the cookies used to make Ice Cream Sandwiches (page 50), or soft and tender, like fruit-filled Orange-Fig Drops (page 61). They are not always made from a traditional dough: Amaretti (page 42), for example, are Italian chewy meringues made from a frothy mixture of egg whites, sugar, and ground almonds.

additions like nuts, raisins, or chocolate chips are incorporated as the final step

STEP 1

Stirring in Ingredients

After mixing the basic dough (see pages 12 to 17), beat in as much of the flour as you can with the mixer. Then, mix in remaining flour and other ingredients with a wooden spoon.

for uniform results, you could use a small, spring-loaded ice cream scoop to shape and drop cookies

STEP 2

Dropping Dough

Scoop up the dough with a small metal spoon. With the back of another spoon or a rubber spatula, push the dough onto a baking sheet.

a chocolate cookie is done if the imprint of your fingertip on its top is barely visible

STEP 3

Testing for Doneness

When done, the cookies will be lightly browned on the bottom. Check by lifting one cookie with a spatula to see the color of its underside. The dough should also feel set. If you're unsure of timing, undercook rather than overcook. The cookies can always go back into the oven for a minute or two.

cookies that are too soft to move should remain on the baking sheet for an extra minute or two to firm up

STEP 4

Cooling on a Rack

After the cookies have finished baking, remove them from the baking sheet with a metal spatula that is big enough to support the whole cookie, and transfer to a wire rack to cool completely.

A delicious after-dinner treat, these sophisticated drop cookies blend rich chocolate with aromatic toasted nuts.

Chocolate-drizzled Praline Cookies

Be careful not to overbake these pecan-laden treats: they are best when nice and chewy. Begin to check for doneness after about 5 minutes.

INGREDIENTS

1/2 cup/4 oz/125 g butter or margarine, softened

1 cup/7 oz/220 g packed brown sugar

1 1/2 teaspoons baking powder

1 egg

2 teaspoons vanilla extract

1 1/2 cups/6 oz/185 g all-purpose (plain) flour

1 cup/4 oz/125 g toasted chopped pecans or walnuts

1/2 cup/3 oz/90 g semisweet (plain) chocolate chips

1 teaspoon shortening

Preparation Time 20 minutes
Baking Time 8 to 10 minutes
Makes about 32 cookies

STEPS AT A GLANCE	Page
Making cookie dough	12–17
Toasting nuts	20
Drizzling chocolate	22
Making drop cookies	32–35

METHOD FOR MAKING CHOCOLATE-DRIZZLED PRALINE COOKIES

In a mixing bowl beat the butter or margarine with an electric mixer on medium to high speed for 30 seconds. Add the brown sugar and baking powder; beat till combined. Beat in the egg and vanilla. Beat in as much of the flour as you can with the mixer. Stir in any remaining flour with a wooden spoon. Stir in the pecans or walnuts.

Drop dough by rounded teaspoons 2 in/5 cm apart onto ungreased baking sheets. Bake in a preheated 375°F/190°C/Gas Mark 4 oven for 8 to 10 minutes, or till bottoms are golden brown. Remove cookies and cool on wire racks.

In a small, heavy-duty plastic bag, combine chocolate chips and shortening. Close bag just above chocolate, then set sealed bag in a bowl of warm water till chocolate is melted. Snip off 1/8 in/3 mm of the corner of the bag. Gently squeeze the bag to pipe chocolate mixture over cookies. Or, melt chocolate and shortening in a saucepan over low heat. Let cool 5 minutes, then drizzle over cookies with a spoon. Let stand till chocolate is set.

Per cookie 107 calories/450 kilojoules, 2 g protein, 13 g carbohydrate, 6 g total fat (2 g saturated), 14 mg cholesterol, 38 mg sodium, 63 mg potassium

Drop Cookies

STEP 1

Melting Chocolate in Bag

Place both chocolate and shortening in a heavy-duty plastic bag and push all to one corner. Tie the bag just above this mixture, then set the bag in a bowl of warm water to melt. Rub to blend the contents.

STEP 2

Snipping Bag

Invert the bag so the tip faces upward. Squeeze a little of the melted mixture away from the tip, then snip off a tiny piece from the corner to create an opening.

You can also pipe icing from a plastic bag. These lacy lines are piped onto Molasses and Ginger Stars (page 166), but you can decorate cookies with dots, daisies, zig-zags, or anything that takes your fancy.

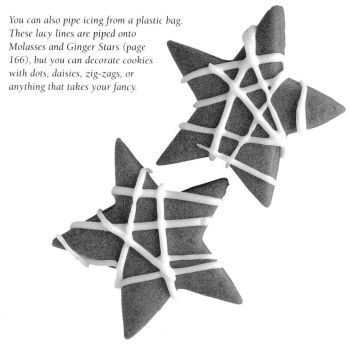

STEP 3

Piping Chocolate
Squeeze the bag gently to pipe out the chocolate in a steady stream. Move back and forth across the cookies, set on a wire rack, to create a network of lines.

About Chocolate

C hocolate comes in various qualities, from over-sweet, cheap-tasting Easter egg chocolate, to superb, rich chocolate that has been conched (kneaded) for up to 100 hours to a smooth, creamy texture. The better the chocolate you use in your recipes, the better the result. It's particularly important to avoid what is called "compound" chocolate. This is cheaper than other chocolates because some of the cocoa butter has been replaced with oil, which dramatically changes the taste and texture of the chocolate. Check the label before you buy. The best chocolate to use in cooking is semisweet (plain) chocolate, unless the recipes specifically asks for another type. Any good quality brand will do.

You can melt chocolate in the top of a double boiler or in the microwave, but be careful not to allow water or steam to get into the chocolate or it will seize up and you'll have to throw it away. (This is why you don't cover chocolate when melting in a microwave oven.) When melting in the microwave, the chocolate will keep its shape and won't appear to have melted. Remove it from the microwave oven and stir it until smooth.

Amaretti

Perfect for a light ending to a big meal, amaretti are puffy confections served frequently in Italy. A cup of espresso or cappuccino would be the perfect complement.

INGREDIENTS

2 egg whites

1 1/4 cups/7 oz/220 g blanched whole almonds

3/4 cup/6 oz/185 g granulated sugar

1/4 teaspoon cream of tartar

1/4 teaspoon almond extract

1/4 cup/1 oz/30 g flaked almonds

Preparation Time 45 minutes
Baking Time 12 to 15 minutes
Cooling Time 30 minutes
Makes about 40 cookies

STEPS AT A GLANCE	Page
Making meringue	**23**
Making drop cookies	**32–35**
Preparing pans & grinding nuts	**45**

*The nutty sweetness of almonds
permeates a classic Italian meringue
drop that is baked until barely browned,
then slowly cooled until dry and crisp.*

In a large mixing bowl let the egg whites stand at room temperature for 30 minutes. Meanwhile, line 2 baking sheets with parchment paper or greaseproof paper. Set aside. In a food processor bowl or blender container process or blend whole almonds with ¼ cup/ 2 oz/60 g of the sugar till almonds are finely ground. Set aside.

Add cream of tartar and almond extract to egg whites. Beat with an electric mixer on medium speed till soft peaks form (tips curl). Gradually add remaining ½ cup/4 oz/125 g sugar, 1 tablespoon at a time, beating on high speed till very stiff peaks form (tips stand straight) and sugar is almost dissolved. Fold in ground almonds.

Drop meringue mixture by rounded teaspoons 1½ in/4 cm apart onto the prepared baking sheets. Sprinkle a few flaked almonds over each cookie. Bake in a preheated 300°F/150°C/Gas Mark 2 oven for 12 to 15 minutes, or till cookies just begin to brown (centers will be soft). Turn off oven. Let cookies dry in oven with the door closed for 30 minutes. Peel cookies from paper. Store in an airtight container in a cool, dry place for up to 1 week.

Per cookie 43 calories/180 kilojoules, 1 g protein, 5 g carbohydrate, 2 g total fat (0 g saturated), 0 mg cholesterol, 3 mg sodium, 38 mg potassium

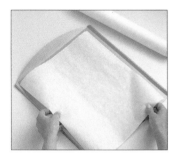

STEP 1

Lining Baking Sheet

Cut a sheet of parchment paper to fit the baking sheet. If your supermarket or kitchenware shop doesn't stock parchment paper, use greaseproof paper.

STEP 2

Grinding Nuts

Put the almonds and ¼ cup/2 oz/60 g of sugar in a food processor or blender. Process or blend until the nuts are finely ground, but still light and dry. Don't overgrind, or the nuts will turn to paste.

All the goodness of a high-energy dried fruit snack is packed into these banana-flavored drops.

Dried Fruit Cookies

If desired, substitute 2½ cups of prepared mix containing dried fruit, nuts, and coconut for the fruits, coconut, and chopped nuts required in this recipe. Be sure to break up any banana chips and whole nuts, and snip any other large pieces of dried fruit into bits.

INGREDIENTS

¾ cup/6 oz/180 g butter or margarine, softened

½ cup/4 oz/125 g granulated sugar

½ cup/3½ oz/105 g packed brown sugar

1 teaspoon baking powder

½ teaspoon baking soda

1 teaspoon ground allspice

2 eggs

1 cup/3 medium mashed bananas

1 teaspoon vanilla extract

1½ cups/6 oz/185 g all-purpose (plain) flour

1½ cups/4½ oz/140 g rolled oats

1 cup/6 oz/185 g mixed dried fruit, chopped

¾ cup/2½ oz/75 g shredded coconut

¾ cup/3 oz/90 g chopped peanuts, walnuts, or pecans

METHOD FOR MAKING DRIED FRUIT COOKIES

Preparation Time 20 minutes
Baking Time 10 to 12 minutes
Makes about 48 cookies

STEPS AT A GLANCE	Page

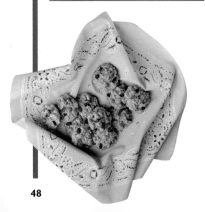

In a large mixing bowl beat the butter or margarine with an electric mixer on medium to high speed for 30 seconds. Add the granulated sugar, brown sugar, baking powder, baking soda, and allspice; beat till combined. Beat in the eggs, mashed bananas, and vanilla. Beat in as much of the flour as you can with the mixer. Stir in any remaining flour with a wooden spoon. Stir in the oats, dried fruit, coconut, and nuts.

Drop dough by rounded tablespoons 2 in/5 cm apart onto ungreased baking sheets. Bake in a preheated 375°F/190°C/Gas Mark 4 oven for 10 to 12 minutes, or till golden brown. Remove cookies and cool on wire racks.

Per cookie 98 calories/410 kilojoules, 2 g protein, 13 g carbohydrate, 5 g total fat (2 g saturated), 16 mg cholesterol, 62 mg sodium, 85 mg potassium

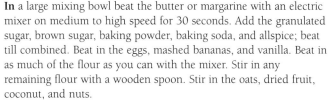

STEP 1

Mashing Bananas

Break up the peeled bananas into several pieces. Place the pieces in a pie plate or shallow bowl and crush with a fork or a vegetable masher.

STEP 2

Chopping Fruit

If using prepared fruit and nut mix, or to chop dried fruit, snip any large pieces of fruit into bits with kitchen scissors. If the blades get sticky, wipe them clean, then spray them with a nonstick cooking spray or grease lightly.

Ice Cream Sandwiches

The ice cream will be a lot easier to work with if you let it soften slightly before packing it into the measuring cup. Let your imagination have free rein when choosing your ice cream flavor.

INGREDIENTS

1 cup/8 oz/250 g butter or margarine, softened

2/3 cup/5 oz/155 g granulated sugar

2 teaspoons baking powder

1/4 teaspoon salt

2 eggs

1/3 cup/4 oz/125 g honey

1 1/2 cups/6 oz/185 g all-purpose (plain) flour

3/4 cup/2 1/2 oz/75 g rolled oats

1/2 cup/3 oz/90 g semisweet (plain) chocolate chips and/or raisins and/or chopped dried fruit

1 qt/1 l vanilla, chocolate, rum raisin, chocolate chip or your choice of ice cream

Ice Cream Sandwiches are a two-in-one dessert: your favorite ice cream plus a double serving of oatmeal cookies rich with your choice of chocolate chips, raisins, and/or dried fruit.

METHOD FOR MAKING ICE CREAM SANDWICHES

Preparation Time 20 minutes
Baking Time 12 to 15 minutes
Freezing Time 1 hour
Makes about 13 cookie sandwiches

STEPS AT A GLANCE	Page
Making cookie dough	**12–17**
Making drop cookies	**32–35**
Chopping fruit	**49**

In a mixing bowl beat the butter or margarine with an electric mixer on medium to high speed for 30 seconds. Add the sugar, baking powder, and salt; beat till combined. Beat in the eggs and honey. Beat in as much of the flour as you can with the mixer. Stir in any remaining flour with a wooden spoon. Stir in the oats and chocolate and/or raisins and/or dried fruit.

Drop dough by rounded tablespoons 3 in/7.5 cm apart onto ungreased baking sheets. Bake in a preheated 375°F/190°C/Gas Mark 4 oven for 12 to 15 minutes, or till golden brown. Cool on baking sheets for 1 minute. Remove cookies and cool on wire racks.

To make each cookie sandwich, pack ice cream into a 3-fl oz/ 80-ml measure or small ramekin and unmold it onto the flat side of a cookie. Top with a second cookie, flat-side down. Press cookies together. Wrap each sandwich in plastic wrap; freeze for about 1 hour, or till ice cream is solid.

Per cookie sandwich 411 calories/172 kilojoules, 5 g protein, 50 g carbohydrate, 22 g total fat (12 g saturated), 84 mg cholesterol, 264 mg sodium, 199 mg potassium

STEPS FOR MAKING SANDWICHES

STEP 1

Molding Ice Cream
Spoon ice cream into 3-fl oz/80-ml measure or ramekin.
Pack down so the ice cream forms a solid disc.

STEP 2

Making Sandwiches
Unmold ice cream onto the flat bottom of a cookie.
Top ice cream with another cookie, flat-side down.

Serve Ice Cream Sandwiches with fresh berries and extra ice cream for an easy dessert. They're also great in winter served singly, straight from the oven with hot poached fruit and thick cream.

STEP 3

Wrapping Cookies
Tightly wrap each sandwich in plastic wrap. Store in an airtight container and freeze until solid.

Triple-Chocolate Cookies

Three different kinds of chocolate in one great cookie! They'll have a more intense flavor if you use the best-quality chocolate you can find. Confectionery shops or gourmet food shops usually have a good selection.

INGREDIENTS

$^1/_2$ cup/4 oz/125 g shortening

$^1/_2$ cup/4 oz/125 g butter or margarine, softened

$^3/_4$ cup/6 oz/185 g granulated sugar

$^3/_4$ cup/6 oz/185 g packed brown sugar

1 teaspoon baking soda

2 eggs

1 teaspoon vanilla extract

$^1/_3$ cup/2 oz/60 g semisweet (plain) chopped chocolate, melted and cooled

$^1/_4$ cup/$^3/_4$ oz/20 g unsweetened cocoa powder

2 cups/8 oz/250 g all-purpose (plain) flour

1$^1/_3$ cups/8 oz/250 g semisweet (plain) chocolate or white chocolate chips

For chocoholics everywhere, here's a triple temptation that is chocolate, chocolate, and more chocolate.

METHOD FOR MAKING TRIPLE-CHOCOLATE COOKIES

Preparation Time 20 minutes
Baking Time 8 to 10 minutes
Makes about 48 cookies

STEPS AT A GLANCE	Page
Making cookie dough	12–17
Melting chocolate	20

In a large mixing bowl beat the shortening and butter or margarine with an electric mixer on medium to high speed for 30 seconds. Add the granulated sugar, brown sugar, and baking soda; beat till combined. Beat in eggs, vanilla, and melted chocolate. Beat in the cocoa powder and as much of the flour as you can with the mixer. Stir in remaining flour with a spoon. Stir in the semisweet (plain) or white chocolate chips.

Drop rounded tablespoons of dough 2 in/5 cm apart onto ungreased baking sheets. Bake in a preheated 375°F/190°C/Gas Mark 4 oven for 8 to 10 minutes, or till tops look dry. Cool on baking sheets for 1 minute; remove cookies and cool on wire racks.

Per cookie 111 calories/466 kilojoules, 1 g protein, 13 g carbohydrate, 6 g total fat (3 g saturated), 14 mg cholesterol, 51 mg sodium, 50 mg potassium

Espresso Meringue Kisses

Espresso powder imparts a distinct coffee flavor to the meringue base of these soft, chewy kisses.

INGREDIENTS

KISSES

2 egg whites

3/4 cup/6 oz/185 g granulated sugar

1 teaspoon instant espresso coffee powder

1 teaspoon vanilla extract

CHOCOLATE GANACHE

1/3 cup/3 fl oz/80 ml heavy (double) cream

2 teaspoons granulated sugar

2 teaspoons butter or margarine

3/4 cup/4 1/2 oz/140 g semisweet (plain) chocolate, chopped

Preparation Time 45 minutes
Baking Time 15 to 20 minutes
Makes about 48 meringues

STEPS AT A GLANCE	Page
Drizzling chocolate	22
Making meringue	23
Making drop cookies	32–35

A delicate web of chocolate crisscrosses espresso-flavored meringues.

METHOD FOR MAKING ESPRESSO MERINGUE KISSES

For kisses, in a medium mixing bowl let egg whites stand at room temperature for 30 minutes. Meanwhile, line 2 baking sheets with parchment paper or greaseproof paper. Set aside. Stir together the sugar and espresso powder. Add vanilla to egg whites. Beat with an electric mixer on medium speed until soft peaks form (tips curl). Gradually add the sugar-espresso powder mixture, 1 tablespoon at a time, beating on high speed just till stiff peaks form (tips stand straight) and sugar is almost dissolved.

Drop mixture by slightly rounded teaspoons 2 in/5 cm apart onto prepared baking sheets. Bake in a preheated 325°F/160°C/Gas Mark 3 oven for 15 to 20 minutes, or till lightly browned. Remove meringues and cool on wire racks.

Meanwhile, for chocolate ganache, in a heavy saucepan stir together the cream, sugar, and butter or margarine. Cook and stir over medium-high heat till sugar is dissolved. Bring mixture to

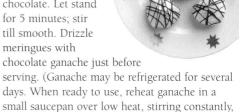

boiling. Meanwhile, place chocolate in a bowl; pour boiling cream mixture over chocolate. Let stand for 5 minutes; stir till smooth. Drizzle meringues with chocolate ganache just before serving. (Ganache may be refrigerated for several days. When ready to use, reheat ganache in a small saucepan over low heat, stirring constantly, till smooth and of drizzling consistency.)

Per meringue 21 calories/88 kilojoules, 0 g protein, 3 g carbohydrate, 1 g total fat (1 g saturated), 3 mg cholesterol, 5 mg sodium, 6 mg potassium

Orange-Fig Drops

**This recipe includes several alternative ingredients. Create your own version by using
a mixture of dried fruits, or use apple juice in place of orange juice or milk.**

INGREDIENTS

COOKIES

1/2 cup/4oz/125 g solid vegetable
shortening

1 teaspoon ground cinnamon

1 teaspoon finely shredded
orange peel

1/2 teaspoon baking soda

1 egg

1/2 cup/4 fl oz/125 ml honey

3 tablespoons orange juice
or milk

2 cups/8 oz/250 g
all-purpose (plain) flour

1 cup/6 oz/185 g
chopped dried
figs or pitted
dates, or raisins

ORANGE ICING

1 cup/4 oz/125 g sifted
confectioners (icing) sugar

1 to 2 tablespoons orange juice

*A drizzle of orange icing provides
a subtle contrast to fruit-filled golden drops.*

METHOD FOR MAKING ORANGE-FIG DROPS

Preparation Time 20 minutes
Baking Time 10 to 12 minutes
Makes about 36 drops

STEPS AT A GLANCE	Page
Making cookie dough	**12–17**
Making drop cookies	**32–35**
Chopping fruit	**49**

For drops, in a mixing bowl beat shortening with an electric mixer on medium to high speed for 30 seconds. Add the cinnamon, orange peel, and baking soda; beat till combined. Beat in the egg, honey, and orange juice or milk till combined. Beat in as much of the flour as you can with the mixer. Stir in any remaining flour with a wooden spoon. Stir in figs, dates, or raisins.

Drop dough by rounded teaspoons 2 in/5 cm apart onto ungreased baking sheets. Bake in a preheated 350°F/180°C/Gas Mark 4 oven for 10 to 12 minutes, or till lightly browned. Remove drops and cool on wire racks.

Meanwhile, for orange icing, in a small mixing bowl stir together confectioners sugar and enough of the orange juice to make an icing of drizzling consistency. Drizzle drops with icing.

Per cookie 91 calories/382 kilojoules, 1 g protein, 15 g carbohydrate, 3 g total fat (1 g saturated), 6 mg cholesterol, 19 mg sodium, 54 mg potassium

Carrot-Raisin Drops

If you want the flavor of carrot cake without the fuss, try these moist, cake-like cookies.
And if you still want something sweet on top, spread each cookie with
a little of your favorite cream cheese frosting recipe.

INGREDIENTS

1 cup/8 oz/250 g butter or margarine, softened

1 cup/7 oz/220 g packed brown sugar

1 teaspoon baking soda

1 teaspoon ground cinnamon

1 teaspoon finely shredded orange peel

1/2 teaspoon ground ginger

1/2 teaspoon ground nutmeg

2 eggs

1 teaspoon vanilla extract

1 1/2 cups/6 oz/185 g all-purpose (plain) flour

1 1/2 cups/6 oz/185 g finely shredded carrots

1 cup/3 oz/90 g rolled oats

1 cup/6 oz/185 g raisins

1/2 cup/2 oz/60 g chopped walnuts or pecans

Golden-brown nuggets get added sweetness from wholesome raisins and vitamin-rich carrots.

METHOD FOR MAKING CARROT-RAISIN DROPS

Preparation Time 20 minutes
Baking Time 6 to 8 minutes
Makes about 72 cookies

In a mixing bowl beat the butter or margarine with an electric mixer on medium to high speed for 30 seconds. Add the brown sugar, baking soda, cinnamon, orange peel, ginger, and nutmeg; beat till combined. Beat in the eggs and vanilla. Beat in as much of the flour as you can with the mixer. Stir in any remaining flour with a wooden spoon. Stir in the carrots, oats, raisins, and nuts.

Drop dough by rounded teaspoons 2 in/5 cm apart onto ungreased baking sheets. Bake in a preheated 375°F/190°C/Gas Mark 4 oven for 6 to 8 minutes, or till golden brown. Remove cookies and cool on wire racks.

Per cookie 63 calories/264 kilojoules, 1 g protein, 8 g carbohydrate, 3 g total fat (2 g saturated), 13 mg cholesterol, 51 mg sodium, 48 mg potassium

Coconut-Macadamia Cookies

Although pecans or almonds are delicious additions to these cookies, there really is no substitute for the mild, buttery taste of macadamias. They usually cost a little more, but we think they're worth it.

INGREDIENTS

1/2 cup/4oz/125 g butter or margarine, softened

1 cup/8 oz/250 g granulated sugar

1/2 teaspoon baking soda

2 eggs

1/2 cup/4 fl oz/125 ml sour cream

1 teaspoon vanilla extract

2 1/2 cups/10 oz/315 g all-purpose (plain) flour

2 cups/6 oz/185 g shredded coconut

1 1/2 cups/8 oz/250 g chopped macadamia nuts, pecans, or almonds

Preparation Time 20 minutes
Baking Time 10 to 12 minutes
Makes about 72 cookies

STEPS AT A GLANCE   Page

Making cookie dough   **12–17**

*Exotic macadamia nuts and chewy coconut give a
tropical accent to easy-to-make drop cookies.
Sour cream gives them a slight tang.*

METHOD FOR MAKING COCONUT-MACADAMIA COOKIES

Drop Cookies

In a mixing bowl beat the butter or margarine with an electric mixer on medium to high speed for 30 seconds. Add the sugar and baking soda; beat till combined. Beat in the eggs, sour cream, and vanilla. Beat in as much of the flour as you can with the mixer. Stir in any remaining flour with a wooden spoon. Stir in the coconut and nuts.

Drop dough by rounded teaspoons 2 in/5 cm apart onto ungreased baking sheets. Bake in a preheated 350°F/180°C/Gas Mark 4 oven for 10 to 12 minutes, or till golden brown. Remove cookies and cool on wire racks.

Per cookie 72 calories/302 kilojoules, 1 g protein, 7 g carbohydrate, 5 g total fat (2 g saturated), 10 mg cholesterol, 26 mg sodium, 25 mg potassium

Bits of toffee brittle make chewy peanut butter drops extra chunky.

Peanut Butter Brittle Drops

If you love peanut butter cookies, try this delicious variation.
The brittle pieces add a terrific crunchy-chewy texture to an old favorite.

INGREDIENTS

1 cup/8 oz/250 g butter or margarine, softened

1¼ cups/9 oz/280 g packed brown sugar

½ cup/4 oz/125 g granulated sugar

½ teaspoon baking soda

2 eggs

1 cup/8 oz/250 g crunchy peanut butter

1 teaspoon vanilla extract

2¼ cups/9 oz/280 g all-purpose (plain) flour

1⅓ cups/8 oz/250 g butter brittle pieces (toffee bits)

Preparation Time 20 minutes
Baking Time 8 to 10 minutes
Makes about 64 cookies

STEPS AT A GLANCE   Page

   Making cookie dough   **12–17**

METHOD FOR MAKING PEANUT BUTTER BRITTLE DROPS

In a large mixing bowl beat the butter or margarine with an electric mixer on medium to high speed for 30 seconds. Add the brown sugar, granulated sugar, and baking soda; beat till combined. Beat in the eggs, peanut butter, and vanilla. Beat in as much of the flour as you can with the mixer. Stir in any remaining flour with a wooden spoon. Stir in butter brittle pieces (toffee bits).

Drop dough by rounded teaspoons 2 in/5 cm apart onto ungreased baking sheets. Bake in a preheated 375°F/190°C/Gas Mark 4 oven for 8 to 10 minutes, or till golden brown. Remove cookies and cool on wire racks.

Per cookie 106 calories/452 kilojoules, 2 g protein, 12 g carbohydrate, 6 g total fat (2 g saturated), 16 mg cholesterol, 84 mg sodium, 53 mg potassium

Frosted Lime Wafers

Finely shredded lime peel and lime juice impart an aromatic, citrus tang to these delicate wafer biscuits, which may also be made with lemons or oranges. Use only the thin colored peel of these fruits, not the bitter white pith beneath.

INGREDIENTS

WAFERS

1 cup/8 oz/250 g butter or margarine, softened

1 cup/8 oz/250 g granulated sugar

1/2 teaspoon baking soda

1/2 teaspoon finely shredded lime peel or 1 teaspoon finely shredded lemon peel

1/3 cup/3 fl oz/80 ml lime juice or lemon juice

2 1/4 cups/9 oz/280 g all-purpose (plain) flour

PASTEL GLAZE

1 cup/4 oz/125 g sifted confectioners (icing) sugar

3 tablespoons butter or margarine, melted

1 to 2 tablespoons lime juice or lemon juice

few drops green or yellow food coloring (optional)

METHOD FOR MAKING FROSTED LIME WAFERS

Preparation Time 20 minutes
Baking Time 10 minutes
Makes about 48 wafers

STEPS AT A GLANCE	Page
Making cookie dough	**12–17**

For wafers, in a mixing bowl beat the butter or margarine with an electric mixer on medium to high speed for 30 seconds. Add the sugar, baking soda, and lime or lemon peel; beat till combined. Beat in the lime or lemon juice. Beat in as much of the flour as you can with the mixer. Stir in any remaining flour with a wooden spoon.

Drop dough by rounded teaspoons 2 in/5 cm apart onto ungreased baking sheets. Bake in a preheated 375°F/190°C/Gas Mark 4 oven for about 10 minutes, or till the edges are beginning to brown. Remove wafers and cool on wire racks.

Meanwhile, for pastel glaze, in a small mixing bowl stir together the confectioners sugar, melted butter or margarine, and enough lime or lemon juice to make a mixture of glazing consistency. If desired, stir in food coloring. Dip tops of wafers in glaze.

Per wafer 84 calories/352 kilojoules, 1 g protein, 10 g carbohydrate, 5 g total fat
(3 g saturated), 12 mg cholesterol, 66 mg sodium, 10 mg potassium

Tart, lime-infused wafers team with fruit sherbet for a refreshing warm-weather dessert.

BAR COOKIES

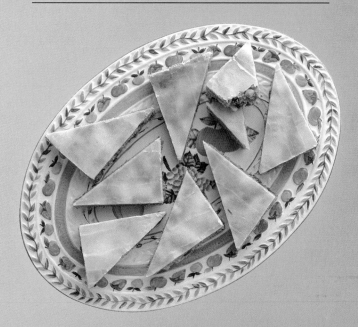

BASIC TOOLS FOR MAKING BAR COOKIES

Some bar cookie recipes are so simple that the batter is mixed in a saucepan, then spooned straight into a baking pan.

baking pan

saucepan

bowl

wooden spoon

rubber spatula

Making Bar Cookies

Mix, bake, serve. Bar cookies are as basic as that. But here basic means easy, not bland or boring. Brownies (like the delectable mocha-flavored ones on page 81) fall into this category, and it's hard to imagine a more delicious dessert or a more popular one. Unlike drop cookies, which are made from a soft dough, bar cookies are made from a fluid batter that needs a baking pan with sides for support. For best results, spread the batter evenly in the pan, so that the finished bars aren't thin and dried out in one corner and thick and undercooked in another. Let the bars cool in the pan, spread with icing, then cut into uniform portions such as squares, rectangles, triangles, or diamonds (see pages 85 and 86 for complete directions). To remove for serving or storage, first run a sharp, thin-bladed knife between the bars and the inside edge of the pan, then lift them out with a spatula that is large enough to support each piece fully.

too much shortening will make the bars gummy; too little will cause them to stick to the pan

STEP 1

Preparing Pan
If the baking pan must be greased, do it as the first step in the recipe. Coat a piece of paper towel or waxed paper with shortening, then apply in a thin, even layer on the bottom and sides of the pan.

stir batter just until mixed or the baked bars will collapse as they cool

STEP 2

Combining Ingredients
If the batter requires a melted ingredient such as chocolate, let it cool slightly before beating in the eggs (or they might curdle). Then gently stir in the remaining ingredients, such as flour, with a wooden spoon.

to create a nicely rounded outside edge, gently spread the batter into the pan corners without letting the spatula touch the sides

STEP 3

Spreading Batter in Pan
Spread the batter in a smooth, even layer across the pan bottom with a rubber spatula or the back of a wooden spoon.

If the pan has sharp corners, like this one, make sure the batter fills each one completely.

STEP 4

Testing for Doneness
Toward the end of baking time, begin to check for doneness. Depending on the recipe, watch for the batter to be set, for the edges to be slightly browned, or for the mixture to pull away slightly from the sides of the pan.

Use a metal icing spatula or the back of a spoon to texture frosting into decorative swirls and ridges. The recipe for Mocha Brownies, shown here, is on page 101.

Making Bar Cookies with a Crust

Multilayered bar cookies have great visual appeal. Although they look complex, they are simple to assemble, which means maximum results for minimum effort. Most bar cookie crusts are quickly tossed together with a pastry blender or a spoon and formed into a layer in the pan with your fingers, like pressed-in pie pastry. The end result might be a rich dough that resembles the base for Coffee-Pecan Triangles (page 113) or one made with cookie crumbs like the crust of Orange Cheesecake Dreams (page 88). If the filling is very liquid, the crust will be prebaked so it won't get soggy. When cutting bar cookies and bar cookies with a crust, you will get the neatest results if you mark off your lines with a simple grid. For either squares or diamonds, use toothpicks as guides for your cutting lines. A perfect square cut in half yields a perfect triangle. For a more generous triangle, cut rectangles in half (see Sour Cream-Date Triangles, page 109).

BASIC TOOLS FOR MAKING BAR COOKIES WITH A CRUST

Use a mixing bowl and pastry blender to prepare cookie crusts, a rubber spatula to transfer batter to a baking pan and to spread fillings, and a sharp knife and toothpicks to cut even bars.

baking pan and cooling rack

mixing bowl

pastry blender

small, sharp knife

rubber spatula

toothpicks

STEPS FOR MAKING BAR COOKIES WITH A CRUST

if the pastry blender gets clogged with butter or margarine, clean it with a rubber spatula or your finger

STEP 1

Cutting in Butter or Margarine
Use a fork to stir together flour, sugar, and salt until thoroughly blended. Cut cold butter or margarine into pieces and cut in with a pastry blender, using an up-and-down motion, until the mixture is crumbly.

smooth the surface with a rubber spatula to remove fingerprints after pressing

STEP 2

Pressing into Pan
Transfer the crust mixture to a baking pan (with a rich dough there is no need to grease the pan first). Push the dough around with your hands until it covers the bottom of the pan in an even layer. Be sure to fill the corners.

if the filling
contains nuts, they
will look best if
chopped into
uniform pieces

STEP 3

Spreading Filling Evenly

While the crust bakes briefly, prepare the filling. Remove the crust from the oven, set the pan on a cooling rack, and pour on the filling. Spread it evenly with a rubber spatula so that every part of the hot crust is covered.

use a ruler to
mark evenly
spaced cutting
lines

STEP 4

Cutting Bar Cookies

Let the cookies cool completely in the pan before cutting them. Then mark cutting lines with toothpicks inserted around the inside edge of the pan. Cut the cookies with a small, sharp knife, using the toothpicks as guides.

STEPS FOR MAKING BAR COOKIES WITH A CRUST

remove from the
pan with a spatula
and separate
into triangles

STEP 5

Cutting Triangles

Make cookie squares according to the directions in step 4; leave them in the pan. To create triangles, cut each square in half diagonally, working from one side of the pan to the other.

the size of the
diamond is
determined
by how far apart
you space the
cutting lines

STEP 6

Cutting Diamonds

As in step 4, place toothpicks around the rim of the pan to mark where you will cut. Divide the cookie lengthwise into long strips, then cut the strips into diamonds by making diagonal cuts from one side of the pan to the other, from toothpick to toothpick.

Cut bar cookies into simple shapes like squares or triangles after baking, cooling and icing. Use a very sharp knife dipped in hot water for clean, straight edges like the ones on these Coffee-Pecan Triangles (page 113). Wipe the knife with a damp paper towel between cuts to get rid of crumbs.

Orange Cheesecake Dreams

A light orange flavor gives these individual cheesecakes an unexpected tang.
If you're making them for a party, garnish each square with a thin half slice of orange.

INGREDIENTS

CRUST

2 cups/6 oz/180 g finely crushed vanilla wafers

1/3 cup/3 oz/90 g butter or margarine, melted

FILLING

1 1/2 cups/11 oz/340 g cream cheese, softened

3/4 cup/6 oz/185 g granulated sugar

2 teaspoons finely shredded orange peel

2 eggs

1/3 cup/3 fl oz/80 ml orange juice

Preparation Time 25 minutes
Baking Time 45 to 50 minutes
Makes about 36 bars

Orange peel and orange juice add a refreshing note to creamy bars. Serve them as the cool finale to a spicy meal.

METHOD FOR MAKING ORANGE CHEESECAKE DREAMS

For crust, in a medium mixing bowl stir together the vanilla wafer crumbs and melted butter or margarine. Set aside one quarter of the crumb mixture. Press remaining mixture evenly into the bottom of a 13x9x2-in/33x23x5-cm baking pan. Bake in a preheated 350°F/180°C/Gas Mark 4 oven for 15 minutes.

For filling, in another mixing bowl beat cream cheese with an electric mixer on medium to high speed for 30 seconds. Beat in sugar and orange peel till combined. Beat in eggs and orange juice on low speed just till combined. Do not overbeat. Spread cream cheese mixture evenly over crust. Sprinkle with reserved crumb mixture.

Bake in the 350°F/180°C/Gas Mark 4 oven for 30 to 35 minutes, or till center appears set. Cool in pan on a rack. Cut into bars; cover and store in the refrigerator.

Per bar 88 calories/369 kilojoules, 1 g protein, 8 g carbohydrate, 6 g total fat (3 g saturated), 29 mg cholesterol, 61 mg sodium, 22 mg potassium

STEP 1

Crushing Wafers

Place vanilla wafers in a heavy-duty plastic bag. Press out all the air, then seal the bag. Crush the cookies into crumbs by rolling over them with a rolling pin.

STEP 2

Sprinkling Crumbs

Spread the cream cheese filling evenly over the partially baked wafer crust with a rubber spatula. Sprinkle the reserved crumb mixture evenly over the filling.

Raspberry jam swirls through a rich chocolate brownie bar that complements after-dinner coffee.

Chocolate-Raspberry Brownies

Raspberry and chocolate are a classic combination, but other flavors of jam
or preserves like cherry, for example, are equally luscious in this recipe.

INGREDIENTS

BROWNIES

1/2 cup/4 oz/125 g butter
or margarine

1/3 cup/2 oz/60 g unsweetened
(bitter) chocolate, chopped

1 cup/8 oz/250 g granulated
sugar

2 eggs

1 teaspoon vanilla extract

1/2 teaspoon almond extract

1 cup/4 oz/125 g all-purpose
(plain) flour

1/3 cup/3 fl oz/80 ml seedless
raspberry jam or preserves

COCOA FROSTING

1 1/2 cups/6 oz/185 g sifted
confectioners (icing) sugar

3 tablespoons unsweetened
cocoa powder

3 tablespoons butter or
margarine, melted

1 teaspoon vanilla extract

1 to 2 tablespoons boiling water

Preparation Time 15 minutes
Baking Time 35 minutes
Makes about 20 brownies

STEPS AT A GLANCE   Page

■ Making bar cookies   78–81

For brownies, in a medium saucepan melt butter or margarine and chocolate over low heat, stirring frequently. Remove from heat. Add the sugar, eggs, vanilla, and almond extract. Using a wooden spoon, lightly beat in flour just till combined. (Do not overbeat or brownies will fall when baked.)

Spread batter into a greased 8x8x2-in/20x20x5-cm baking pan. Spoon raspberry jam in dollops over batter; run a knife through batter several times to achieve a marbled effect. Bake in a preheated 350°F/180°C/Gas Mark 4 oven for about 35 minutes, or till set. Cool in pan on a rack.

Meanwhile, for cocoa frosting, in a medium mixing bowl stir together the confectioners sugar, cocoa powder, melted butter or margarine, and vanilla. Stir in enough of the boiling water to make a frosting of spreading consistency. Spread over cooled brownies. If desired, score frosting with the tines of a fork. Cut into bars.

Per brownie 187 calories/785 kilojoules, 2 g protein, 27 g carbohydrate, 8 g total fat (5 g saturated), 39 mg cholesterol, 81 mg sodium, 45 mg potassium

STEPS FOR SWIRLING BATTER AND SCORING FROSTING

STEP 1

Adding Jam or Preserves
Prepare the batter and spread it in the greased baking pan. Spoon seedless raspberry jam or preserves at even intervals across the surface.

STEP 2

Marbling Jam or Preserves
Insert a small metal spatula or knife in the center of one spoonful of jam or preserves. Drag through the jam with a swirling motion to pull it through the batter until you reach another dollop of jam. Continue swirling the remaining jam to create a marble pattern.

STEP 3

Scoring Frosting
Spread frosting evenly over the entire surface of the batter. Using just enough pressure to make score marks, pull the tines of a fork through the frosting on the diagonal.

Hazelnut Toffee Bars

These toffee confections are like melt-in-the-mouth homemade candies.
Sprinkle broken toffee or brittle bits over the top instead of nuts for a decadent touch.

INGREDIENTS

1 cup/8 oz/250 g butter or margarine, softened

1/2 cup/3 1/2 oz/105 g packed brown sugar

1/2 teaspoon salt

3 tablespoons milk

1 teaspoon vanilla extract

1 1/2 cups/6 oz/185 g all-purpose (plain) flour

1 cup/4 oz/125 g finely chopped hazelnuts, pecans, or walnuts

9 oz/280 g good-quality milk chocolate bars

Preparation Time 20 minutes
Baking Time 20 to 25 minutes
Makes about 36 bars

STEPS AT A GLANCE	Page
■ Making bar cookies	**78–81**

*These cookies are based
on a toffee crust, and chocolate
bars make a simple icing.*

In a medium mixing bowl beat the butter or margarine with an electric mixer on medium to high speed for 30 seconds. Add the brown sugar and salt and beat till combined. Beat in the milk and vanilla. Beat in as much of the flour as you can with the mixer. Stir in any remaining flour with a wooden spoon. Stir in half the hazelnuts, pecans, or walnuts.

Spread batter in a greased 13x9x2-in/33x23x5-cm baking pan. Bake in a preheated 350°F/180°C/Gas Mark 4 oven for 20 to 25 minutes, or till lightly browned around the edges.

Immediately place chocolate bars on top of the hot crust. Let stand for 2 to 3 minutes, or till chocolate is melted. Spread chocolate evenly over crust. Sprinkle remaining nuts over chocolate. Cool in pan on a rack. Cut into bars.

Per bar 133 calories/558 kilojoules, 2 g protein, 11 g carbohydrate, 9 g total fat (5 g saturated), 14 mg cholesterol, 100 mg sodium, 63 mg potassium

Bar Cookies

STEP 1

Adding Chocolate

Bake the crust until lightly browned around the edges and remove from the oven. Immediately arrange unwrapped milk-chocolate bars in two even rows over the hot crust.

STEP 2

Spreading Chocolate

Wait for the chocolate to melt, then spread the melted bars over the crust with an icing knife or small spatula, making some swirls and ridges for texture.

Coffee and chocolate always enhance each other. Mocha Brownies are the delicious proof.

Mocha Brownies

**These quick-to-prepare brownies are an easy dessert
to whip up when unexpected guests arrive.**

INGREDIENTS

BROWNIES

1 cup/8 oz/250 g granulated sugar

1/2 cup/4 oz/125 g butter or margarine

1/3 cup/1 oz/30 g unsweetened cocoa powder

1 teaspoon instant coffee granules

2 eggs

1 teaspoon vanilla extract

2/3 cup/3 oz/90 g all-purpose (plain) flour

1/2 teaspoon baking powder

1/4 teaspoon salt

1/2 cup/2 oz/60 g chopped walnuts

FROSTING

3 tablespoons butter or margarine, softened

1/4 cup/3/4 oz/20 g unsweetened cocoa powder

2 cups/8 oz/250 g sifted confectioners (icing) sugar

2 to 3 tablespoons milk

1/2 teaspoon vanilla extract

METHOD FOR MAKING MOCHA BROWNIES

Preparation Time 20 minutes
Baking Time 25 minutes
Makes about 12 brownies

STEPS AT A GLANCE   Page

For brownies, in a medium saucepan combine granulated sugar, butter or margarine, cocoa powder, and coffee granules. Cook and stir over medium heat till butter or margarine melts. Remove from heat; cool for 5 minutes. Add eggs and vanilla. Beat lightly by hand just till combined. Stir in the flour, baking powder, and salt. Stir in walnuts. Spread the batter in a greased 9x9x2-in/23x23x5-cm baking pan. Bake in a preheated 350°F/180°C/Gas Mark 4 oven for 25 minutes, or till set. Cool in pan on a rack.

For frosting, in a mixing bowl beat butter or margarine till fluffy. Add cocoa powder. Gradually add 1 cup/4 oz/125 g of the confectioners sugar, beating well. Slowly beat in 2 tablespoons of the milk and the vanilla. Slowly beat in remaining sugar. Beat in additional milk, if necessary, to make a frosting of spreading consistency.

Spread frosting over cooled brownies. Cut into bars.

Per brownie 308 calories/1293 kilojoules, 4 g protein, 41 g carbohydrate, 15 g fat (7 g saturated), 64 mg cholesterol, 164 mg sodium, 58 mg potassium

For a more decadent brownie, sprinkle lavishly with chopped walnuts or chocolate chips. Or, serve with fresh fruit: strawberries, raspberries and orange segments have a particular affinity with chocolate.

These chewy golden bars are like thick chocolate chip cookies made with chopped chocolate and toasted nuts.

Blonde Brownies

**These are "Blondies", with a melted chocolate and toasted nut topping.
Leave the skin on the nuts and chop them coarsely.**

INGREDIENTS

2 cups/14 oz/440 g packed
brown sugar

2/3 cup/5 oz/155 g butter
or margarine

2 eggs

2 teaspoons vanilla extract

2 cups/8 oz/250 g all-purpose
(plain) flour

1 teaspoon baking powder

1/4 teaspoon baking soda

1 cup/6 oz/185 g chopped sweet
cooking chocolate

2/3 cup/4 oz/125 g toasted
chopped hazelnuts or almonds

Preparation Time 20 minutes
Baking Time 35 minutes
Makes about 36 brownies

STEPS AT A GLANCE	Page
Toasting nuts	20

METHOD FOR MAKING BLONDE BROWNIES

In a large saucepan heat brown sugar and butter or margarine, stirring constantly till sugar dissolves. Remove pan from heat. Cool slightly. Add eggs, one at a time, and the vanilla. Beat slightly by hand just till combined. Stir in flour, baking powder, and baking soda.

Spread batter in a greased 13x9x2-in/33x23x5-cm baking pan. Sprinkle with chopped chocolate and hazelnuts or almonds.

Bake in a preheated 350°F/180°C/Gas Mark 4 oven for 35 minutes. Cut into bars while still warm; cool bars completely in pan.

Per brownie 142 calories/596 kilojoules, 1 g protein, 20 g carbohydrate, 7 g total fat (3 g saturated), 21 mg cholesterol, 56 mg sodium, 77 mg potassium

If you're feeling self-indulgent, these brownies make a fantastic sundae when topped with ice cream, hot chocolate sauce, and some extra chopped nuts. Garnish with fresh fruit.

About Hazelnuts

Hazelnuts, also known as cobnuts or filberts, are crisp and sweet. Their round, grape-like shape makes them ideal for candying whole, and using as a decoration for cookies. Or, they can be sliced by hand with a small serrated knife (leave their skin on for color contrast and added flavor) and used as an attractive and delicious topping. Ground hazelnuts can replace flour in some recipes and will result in very moist cookies. Hazelnuts may be used whole or chopped, with their skin on, or they may be toasted and skinned (see pages 20 and 21).

When toasting hazelnuts, stir often, to make sure they don't burn. Their skins are thinner than almonds, and don't slip off so easily. If you have trouble removing the skins using the technique on page 21, try this method: after toasting the nuts, put them into a paper bag, or wrap in a clean cloth and rub them against one another. If you want to remove the skins without toasting the nuts, put them in a bowl and pour boiling water over them. Leave for about 5 minutes, drain, and remove the skins with a knife.

Always store hazelnuts in their skins — they will keep much longer. Place them in an airtight container and store them in the refrigerator.

Sour Cream-Date Triangles

Fruit-and-nut triangles are aromatic with spices and the rich flavor of brown sugar.
They suit a dessert tray or afternoon tea equally well.

INGREDIENTS

BARS

2 cups/8 oz/250 g all-purpose (plain) flour

1½ cups/11 oz/345 g packed brown sugar

1 teaspoon baking powder

1 teaspoon ground cinnamon

½ teaspoon baking soda

½ teaspoon salt

2 eggs

1 cup/8 oz/250 g butter or margarine, softened

½ cup/4 fl oz/125 ml sour cream

1⅓ cups/8 oz/250 g chopped pitted dates or 1⅓ cups/8 oz/250 g raisins

½ cup/2 oz/60 g chopped walnuts or pecans

GLAZE

1½ cups/6 oz/185 g sifted confectioners (icing) sugar

3 tablespoons butter or margarine, melted

1 tablespoon lemon juice

1 to 2 tablespoons water

few drops yellow food coloring (optional)

METHOD FOR MAKING SOUR CREAM-DATE TRIANGLES

Preparation Time 25 minutes
Baking Time 20 to 25 minutes
Makes about 36 triangles

STEPS AT A GLANCE	Page
■ Making bar cookies	78–81

For bars, in a medium mixing bowl stir together the flour, brown sugar, baking powder, cinnamon, baking soda, and salt. Beat in the eggs, butter or margarine, and sour cream till thoroughly combined. Stir in the dates or raisins and walnuts or pecans. Spread the batter in a greased 15x10x1-in/37.5x25x2.5-cm baking pan.

Bake in a preheated 350°F/180°C/Gas Mark 4 oven for 20 to 25 minutes, or till a wooden toothpick inserted near the center comes out clean. Cool in pan on a rack.

For glaze, in a medium mixing bowl stir together the confectioners sugar, melted butter or margarine, lemon juice, and enough water to make a mixture of glazing consistency. If desired, tint glaze with food coloring. Spread glaze over cooled bars. Cut into rectangles, then halve rectangles diagonally to make triangles.

Per serving 164 calories/688 kilojoules, 2 g protein, 23 g carbohydrate, 8 g total fat (4 g saturated), 29 mg cholesterol, 117 mg sodium, 99 mg potassium

*A translucent lemony
glaze covers rich, spicy
fruit-filled bars, cut into
generous triangles.*

A meltingly tender crust is hidden beneath a glossy nut-covered topping that turns a rich brown as it bakes.

Coffee-Pecan Triangles

These rich, creamy bars are simple to make. Follow the instructions on page 86, step 5, to cut them into neat triangles.

INGREDIENTS

CRUST

2 cups/8 oz/250 g all-purpose (plain) flour

1/2 cup/2 oz/60 g sifted confectioners (icing) sugar

1/2 teaspoon salt

3/4 cup/6 oz/180 g cold butter or margarine

Preparation Time 25 minutes
Baking Time 30 minutes
Makes about 48 triangles

FILLING

2 eggs

1/2 cup/3 1/2 oz/105 g packed brown sugar

1 cup/4 oz/125 g chopped pecans

1/2 cup/4 fl oz/125 ml honey

1/4 cup/2 oz/60 g butter or margarine, melted

2 tablespoons light (single) cream

1 teaspoon instant coffee granules

1 teaspoon vanilla extract

For crust, in a medium mixing bowl stir together the flour, confectioners sugar, and salt. Cut in butter or margarine till crumbly. Press mixture evenly into the bottom of a 13x9x2-in/33x23x5-cm baking pan. Bake in a preheated 350°F/180°C/Gas Mark 4 oven for 10 minutes.

Meanwhile, for filling, in another mixing bowl beat eggs slightly. Stir in the brown sugar, pecans, honey, and melted butter or margarine. Stir together the light cream, coffee granules, and vanilla till coffee granules dissolve. Stir into pecan mixture. Spread mixture evenly over hot crust.

Bake in the 350°F/180°C/Gas Mark 4 oven for 20 minutes more, or till set. Cool in pan on a rack. Cut into squares, then halve squares diagonally to make triangles.

Per triangle 94 calories/394 kilojoules, 1 g protein, 10 g carbohydrate, 6 g total fat (2 g saturated), 19 mg cholesterol, 72 mg sodium, 32 mg potassium

Soft Lemon Drops

This lemon-flavored cookie has a soft texture and a lemony glaze.

Preparation time: 30 minutes • **Baking time:** 10 minutes per pan

Cookie

  1 cup sugar
  ½ cup LAND O LAKES® Butter, softened*
  ¼ cup LAND O LAKES® Half & Half
    2 eggs
  2 tsp grated lemon peel
  ½ tsp lemon extract

  2 ½ cups all-purpose flour
    1 tsp baking powder
    ½ tsp salt

Glaze

    1 cup powdered sugar
  1 to 2 tbsp lemon juice

- Heat oven to 350°F. Combine sugar and butter in large bowl. Beat at medium speed, scraping bowl often, until creamy. Add half & half, eggs, lemon peel and lemon extract; continue beating until well mixed. Reduce speed to low; add flour, baking powder and salt. Beat until well mixed.
- Drop dough by rounded teaspoonfuls 2 inches apart onto Reynolds® Parchment Paper-lined (or greased) cookie sheets. Bake for 10 to 12 minutes or until lightly browned. Cool completely.
- Combine powdered sugar and enough lemon juice for desired glazing consistency in small bowl. Glaze cooled cookies. Makes 3 dozen cookies.

*Substitute LAND O LAKES® Soft Baking Butter with Canola Oil right from the refrigerator.

Soft Lemon Drops

Apricot Macaroon Bars

Most apricot bars have a cookie crust, but these are a cross between a light coconut cake and macaroons. You can use other dried fruits for a different flavor.

INGREDIENTS

CRUST

³/₄ cup/6 oz/185 g butter or margarine, softened

1 cup/8 oz/250 g granulated sugar

2 eggs

¹/₄ teaspoon almond extract

1¹/₂ cups/6 oz/185 g all-purpose (plain) flour

1 cup/3 oz/90 g shredded coconut

FILLING

1¹/₂ cups/6 oz/185 g dried apricots, chopped

1 cup/8 fl oz/250 ml water

¹/₂ cup/3¹/₂ oz/105 g packed brown sugar

¹/₂ teaspoon vanilla extract

¹/₃ cup/1 oz/30 g toasted shredded coconut

METHOD FOR MAKING APRICOT MACAROON BARS

Preparation Time 30 minutes
Baking Time 35 minutes
Makes about 36 bars

STEPS AT A GLANCE	Page
Chopping fruit	49
Making bar cookies with a crust	82–87

For crust, in a large mixing bowl beat butter or margarine with an electric mixer on medium to high speed for 30 seconds. Add the granulated sugar and beat till combined. Beat in eggs and almond extract. Beat in as much of the flour as you can with the mixer. Stir in any remaining flour with a wooden spoon. Stir in coconut. Spread the batter into a well-greased 13x9x2-in/33x23x5-cm baking pan. Bake in a preheated 350°F/180°C/Gas Mark 4 oven for 25 minutes.

Meanwhile, for filling, in a saucepan combine the dried apricots and water. Bring to boiling; reduce heat. Simmer, covered, for 7 to 8 minutes, or till apricots are tender. Stir in brown sugar. Cook and stir till sugar is dissolved. Remove from heat and stir in vanilla. Spoon over hot crust. Sprinkle evenly with toasted coconut.

Bake in the 350°F/180°C/Gas Mark 4 oven for 10 minutes more, or till a toothpick inserted near the center comes out clean. Cool in pan on a rack. Cut into bars.

Per bar 111 calories/466 kilojoules, 1 g protein, 16 g carbohydrate, 5 g total fat (3 g saturated), 22 mg cholesterol, 50 mg sodium, 95 mg potassium

*Dried apricots and coconut make these
tender bars incredibly moist.
The coconut on top is
toasted for extra flavor.*

Create a lattice effect by piping the topping over the bars in diagonal lines, first in one direction, then the other.

Pumpkin Spice Bars

Don't wait until winter to make these soft bars; they're just as good with a glass
of lemonade as with a cup of hot cider. Look for candied ginger
in supermarkets and gourmet shops.

INGREDIENTS

BARS

1 1/2 cups/6 oz/185 g all-purpose
(plain) flour

1 cup/7 oz/220 g packed
brown sugar

1/2 cup/4 oz/125 g granulated sugar

2 teaspoons baking powder

1/4 teaspoon baking soda

2 teaspoons finely chopped
candied (crystallized) ginger or
1/2 teaspoon ground ginger

1 teaspoon ground cinnamon

1/4 teaspoon salt

2 eggs

1 cup/8 oz/250 g cooked mashed
pumpkin

3/4 cup/4 1/2 oz/140 g raisins

1/2 cup/4 fl oz/125 ml cooking oil

TOPPING

1/2 cup/3 oz/90 g white chocolate,
chopped

1 teaspoon solid vegetable
shortening

METHOD FOR MAKING PUMPKIN SPICE BARS

Preparation Time 25 minutes
Baking Time 15 to 20 minutes
Makes about 48 bars

STEPS AT A GLANCE	Page
Piping chocolate	22
Making bar cookies	78–81

For bars, in a large mixing bowl stir together the flour, brown sugar, granulated sugar, baking powder, baking soda, candied or ground ginger, cinnamon, and salt. In another mixing bowl beat the eggs slightly. Stir in the pumpkin, raisins, and oil. Stir pumpkin mixture into flour mixture.

Spread batter into an ungreased 15x10x1-in/37.5x25x2.5-cm baking pan. Bake in a preheated 350°F/180°C/Gas Mark 4 oven for 15 to 20 minutes, or till a wooden toothpick inserted near the center comes out clean. Cool in pan on a rack.

For topping, in a small, heavy-duty plastic bag combine white chocolate and shortening. Close bag just above ingredients, then set sealed bag in a bowl of warm water till contents are melted. Snip ¼ in/6 mm from one corner of bag. Squeeze topping from bag over bars in a crisscross design. Cut bars before topping is completely set.

Per bar 81 calories/340 kilojoules, 1 g protein, 13 g carbohydrate, 3 g total fat (1 g saturated), 9 mg cholesterol, 22 mg sodium, 61 mg potassium

Chocolate-Coconut Meringue Bars

The coconut and meringue add crunch to the brownie crust. These are best eaten the first day, although they will keep overnight in the refrigerator.

INGREDIENTS

BARS

3/4 cup/6 oz/180 g butter or margarine

1/2 cup/3 oz/90 g semisweet (plain) chocolate, chopped

1 cup/7 oz/220 g packed brown sugar

2 egg yolks

1 teaspoon vanilla extract

1 3/4 cups/7 oz/220 g all-purpose (plain) flour

1/4 teaspoon salt

1 cup/3 oz/90 g shredded coconut

MERINGUE

2 egg whites

1/2 cup/4 oz/125 g granulated sugar

1/2 cup/2 1/2 oz/75 g finely chopped almonds or pecans

2 tablespoons shredded coconut

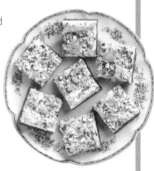

METHOD FOR MAKING CHOCOLATE-COCONUT MERINGUE BARS

Preparation Time 25 minutes
Baking Time 40 to 45 minutes
Makes about 16 bars

For bars, in a medium, heavy saucepan heat butter or margarine and chocolate over medium heat till melted, stirring frequently. Stir in the brown sugar, egg yolks, and vanilla. Using a wooden spoon, beat lightly just till combined. (Do not overbeat or bars will fall when baked.) Stir in the flour, salt, and coconut. Spread batter in a greased 9x9x2-in/ 23x23x5-cm baking pan. Bake in a preheated 350°F/180°C/Gas Mark 4 oven for 25 minutes.

Meanwhile, for meringue, in a medium mixing bowl beat the egg whites with an electric mixer on high speed till soft peaks form (tips curl). Gradually beat in the granulated sugar, 1 tablespoon at a time, till stiff peaks form (tips stand up) and sugar is almost dissolved. Spread over hot crust. Sprinkle with chopped almonds and coconut.

Bake in the 350°F/180°C/Gas Mark 4 oven for 15 to 20 minutes more, or till meringue is set and lightly browned. Cool in pan on a rack. Cut into bars.

Per bar 280 calories/1176 kilojoules, 4 g protein, 35 g carbohydrate, 15 g total fat (8 g saturated), 50 mg cholesterol, 148 mg sodium, 142 mg potassium

The meringue layer is spread over the hot brownie crust, sprinkled with chopped nuts and coconut, and baked until set and golden.

CUTOUT COOKIES

Making Cutout Cookies

A buttery cookie shaped like a little boy, or a cookie kitten with its tail tucked under, is more than just a confection. It is an edible example of cookie artistry. Some cookie shapes are formed with a cutter, some are created with a ruler and knife. All are made from a rich, pliable dough that must be chilled for easier handling, an advantage because it can be made up to 1 week ahead. When ready, roll it out into a thin, even sheet. Then the fun begins: There are countless cookie cutter shapes for every occasion. Be sure to select cutters with sharp edges and patterns that are free of tiny details such as little ears or skinny tails that might break off as the dough drops from the cutter. To make the most out of a piece of dough, view it like an uncut puzzle and space the shapes as close together as you can. Knead the scraps and reroll to use up the remaining dough. After baking, let the cookies cool briefly on the baking sheet, then transfer to a wire cooling rack with a large spatula that will fully support each. Let hot baking sheets cool before using them again, or the dough will spread out of shape.

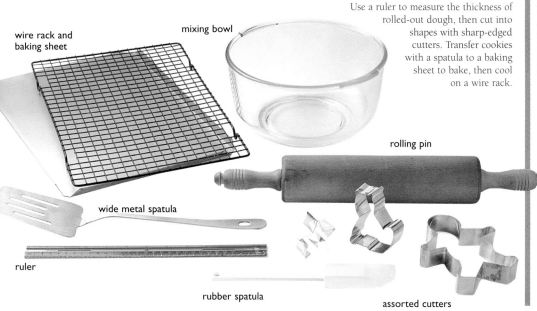

Use a ruler to measure the thickness of rolled-out dough, then cut into shapes with sharp-edged cutters. Transfer cookies with a spatula to a baking sheet to bake, then cool on a wire rack.

wire rack and baking sheet

mixing bowl

rolling pin

wide metal spatula

ruler

rubber spatula

assorted cutters

STEPS FOR MAKING CUTOUT COOKIES

chilled dough is easier to roll and won't stick to the rolling pin

STEP 1

Chilling Dough

Prepare the dough and divide it into two equal pieces; flatten slightly. Tear off two large squares of plastic wrap. Tightly wrap each piece of dough in plastic wrap and chill until the dough is easy to handle, about 1 to 3 hours, depending on the recipe.

well-wrapped dough can be stored in the refrigerator for up to 1 week

the thickness may differ depending on the recipe

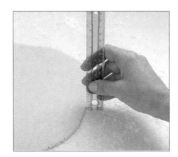

STEP 2

Measuring Thickness

On a lightly floured surface, roll out one portion of dough ⅛ in/3 mm thick (keep the remaining half chilled until needed). Measure the dough with a ruler to check that it is of uniform thickness.

if desired, peel away the dough scraps around the cookie shapes first to make them easier to reach

a floured cutting edge makes a straighter cut

STEP 3

Cutting Out Cookies

Dip the cutting edge of the cookie cutter into flour. Set the cutter on the dough. Press straight down with equal pressure all the way around so that all parts of the pattern are cut out.

if the cookie sticks to the cutter, hold the cutter over the baking sheet and gently tap one edge on the sheet to dislodge the dough

STEP 4

Moving Cookie to Sheet

Slide a large, wide spatula under the cookie and transfer it to a baking sheet. Leave some room between the shapes because they will expand as they bake.

light kneading blends the dough without making it tough

STEP 5

Rerolling Scraps

After as many cookies as possible have been cut out of the dough, gather the scraps with your lightly floured hands and gently knead the dough. Then reroll the dough ⅛ in/3 mm thick and cut out more cookies.

sugar cookies and most other cutouts brown lightly only on the bottom (the edges are firm, but not browned)

STEP 6

Testing for Doneness

If you think the cookies are ready to remove from the oven, check by lifting one with a spatula to see the color on its underside. Transfer to a wire rack to cool.

Even without decoration, cookie shapes have a whimsical charm, but when they're iced like these Holiday Cookies, page 160, they're irresistible.

BASIC TOOLS FOR BUILDING COTTAGE

You will need the tools shown here, plus the items listed on page 136, to build a gingerbread cottage.

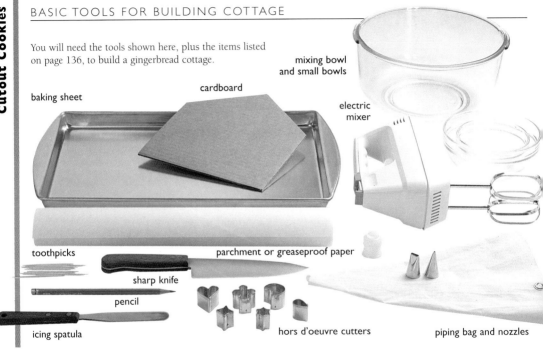

mixing bowl
and small bowls

cardboard

baking sheet

electric
mixer

toothpicks

parchment or greaseproof paper

sharp knife

pencil

icing spatula

hors d'oeuvre cutters

piping bag and nozzles

Making a Gingerbread Cottage

Attention budding architects: design your dream house, guaranteed ready for immediate enjoyment! Gingerbread may not be the most permanent building material, but it is certainly the most delicious. For many families, baking and decorating such a structure is a treasured holiday tradition. It all begins with a basic foundation of gingerbread sheets. Walls and roof are cut out around a paper template, then "glued" together with white royal icing that forms a very tight bond after it dries. Decorations, shutters, trees, and a chimney are created freehand. And you can actually eat it.

Gingerbread construction has two schools of thought: a simple building, elaborately embellished, or an elaborate structure, simply finished. To get you started, we have designed a charming cottage that is neither fussy nor too plain. It requires a minimum of pieces and is ready to decorate with icing, embossing, and candies of every color. Enlarge the template pieces on page 136 to cut out parts of the cottage, then follow the recipe and steps for a Christmas cottage so delightful it will be difficult to persuade anyone in the family to take the first bite.

Gingerbread Dough & Icing

INGREDIENTS

DOUGH

8 cups/2 lb/1 kg all-purpose (plain) flour

2 teaspoons ground ginger

1 1/2 teaspoons ground cinnamon

1 teaspoon ground cloves

2 1/4 cups/18 oz/560 g solid vegetable shortening

2 cups/1 lb/500 g granulated sugar

2 eggs

1 cup/8 fl oz/250 ml light molasses or golden syrup

2/3 cup/5 fl oz/160 ml light corn syrup or golden syrup

ICING

3 egg whites

4 cups/1 lb/500 g confectioners (icing) sugar, sifted

1 teaspoon vanilla extract

1/2 teaspoon cream of tartar

Preparation Time 4 hours
Baking Time 10 to 12 minutes
Makes 6 portions dough and 24 fl oz/750 ml icing

For the dough, in a large mixing bowl, combine flour, ginger, cinnamon, and cloves; set aside.

In another bowl, beat shortening and sugar together with an electric mixer till fluffy. Add eggs, and molasses and corn syrup or golden syrup. Beat till combined. Add flour mixture gradually to shortening mixture. Beat well. If necessary, stir in the last 2 cups/8 oz/500 g of the flour mixture with a wooden spoon; knead dough till smooth. Divide dough into 6 equal portions. Cover.

Enlarge the template pieces for the house as directed in step 1 on page 137. Cut out template pieces on parchment or greaseproof paper. Grease the back of a 15x10x1-in/37.5x25x2.5-cm baking pan or a large baking sheet. Roll out one portion of the dough to a 1/4-in/6-mm thickness on the greased pan. Place a template piece on dough. Cut around piece with a knife. Remove excess dough. Mark the windows, doors, and wall or roof texture as shown in step 2 on page 137.

Leave dough on pan and bake in a preheated 375°F/190°C/Gas Mark 4 oven for 10 to 12 minutes, or till edges are browned. Place template piece on gingerbread and recut if necessary to make straight edges. Let cool 5 minutes on pan. Transfer to a wire rack and cool. Repeat with remaining dough and templates till all the house pieces are baked. Lightly knead and roll out scraps; cut out rectangular shutters, if desired. Bake as directed. Cool gingerbread pieces completely before beginning to assemble cottage. If you allow the pieces to dry overnight, they will be even firmer and better for construction.

For the icing, in a large mixing bowl, combine egg whites, confectioners sugar, vanilla extract, and cream of tartar. Beat with an electric mixer on high speed for 7 to 10 minutes, or till the mixture becomes very stiff. Use at once. Cover any icing in bowl at all times with plastic wrap. You will need to make extra icing to decorate the garden.

MATERIALS FOR MAKING
A GINGERBREAD COTTAGE

To make the gingerbread cottage, you will need the following ingredients and materials:

- One recipe Gingerbread Dough & Icing
- Peppermint sticks and assorted candies, sugar cubes, nuts, and sprinkles for decoration
- Confectioners sugar
- Food coloring
- Ice cream cones
- Plastic or wooden board for a base
- Parchment paper or greaseproof paper
- Cardboard
- Pencil
- Baking sheet
- Mixing bowls, mixer, and small bowls
- Chef's knife
- Icing spatula
- Piping bag and nozzles
- Hors d'oeuvre cutters

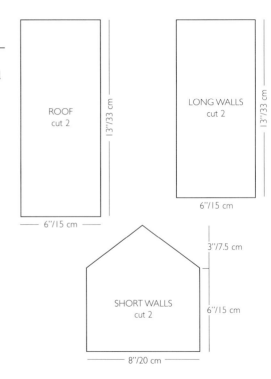

ROOF
cut 2

13"/33 cm

6"/15 cm

LONG WALLS
cut 2

13"/33 cm

6"/15 cm

SHORT WALLS
cut 2

3"/7.5 cm

6"/15 cm

8"/20 cm

the moist dough will hold the paper template in place while you cut out the gingerbread pieces

STEP 1

Cutting Cottage Shapes

Enlarge the templates opposite to full size on parchment paper or greaseproof paper. Place 1 portion of dough at a time on the back of a 15x10x1-in/37.5x25x2.5-cm baking sheet. Roll the dough slightly larger than the template piece and cut around the template with a knife. Slide excess dough away from main section; remove and wrap in plastic. Bake and repeat with each remaining portion of dough.

use small holes created by a toothpick as guides when you draw the door and windows with icing

STEP 2

Marking Windows and Doors

Mark placement of windows and doors by poking a toothpick through the corners in the paper template. Remove the template. Score window and door outlines with a knife between corner marks.

leave a margin of
dough around the
cutouts so they
aren't hidden by
the overhang of
the roof

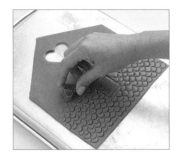

STEP 3

Marking Texture in Walls

Texture walls with a small heart cutter, if desired. Use a
1½-in/4-cm heart cutter to cut the door and end-wall
windows. Score roof pieces with an hors d'oeuvre cutter
or knife.

egg whites will
beat to greater
volume if they are
at room
temperature
rather than cold

STEP 4

Beating Icing to Stiff Peaks

Beat egg whites, icing sugar, vanilla, and cream of tartar
on high speed with an electric mixer until the icing is
glossy and stands in stiff, straight peaks when the
beaters are lifted.

to make shutters, reroll scraps and cut
rectangles freehand; make heart-shaped
perforations with a tiny cutter

STEP 5

Outlining with Icing
Glue the shutters to the house with
dabs of icing. Place icing in a piping
bag with a small, round writing
nozzle. Use the icing to outline the
windows, including the panes, and
other architectural features.

STEP 6

Decorating with Candies
Select candies that won't overwhelm
the more subtle textures on the
walls and roof. Study each side of
the house before proceeding. Put
candies in place, but don't use icing
"glue" just yet. If you are pleased
with the effect, then attach the
candies with the icing.

the icing will stay fluid because it is
protected from air in the piping bag

STEP 7

Finishing Walls
Continue to apply candies on all
four walls until you are satisfied
with the overall design. Check that
each candy is firmly attached. If any
are loose when gently prodded,
remove them. Pipe on more icing,
then put back in place.

STEP 8

Assembling House

Cut one short wall template out of cardboard for support; set aside. Mark a 12x8-in/30x20-cm baseline on a large plastic or wooden board. Pipe icing along the bottom and side edges of a short wall. Position on the baseline and support it with cans of food, if necessary.

For the long wall, pipe icing on the bottom edge and on the back along the two short sides. Place long wall on the baseline next to the short wall. Pipe icing along the bottom and side edges of remaining short wall. Position on the baseline.

Pipe icing along the bottom and side edges of the cardboard support wall and place it inside the house, halfway between the short walls.

For the remaining long wall, pipe icing on the bottom edge and on the back along the two short sides. Place the wall in position. Add extra icing as necessary to make strong corners. Let dry several hours or overnight before adding the roof.

For the roof, pipe a thick row of icing across the top edge of one long wall and along the adjoining top edges of each short wall, including the cardboard support wall. Position one roof section and hold until set. Repeat on the other side with the remaining roof section.

Reserve remaining icing in a covered bowl and use to build the chimney and create trees. If you want to decorate the garden, you will need to prepare a second batch of icing.

the nuts should completely cover the sugar cubes from bottom to top

STEP 9

Building the Chimney

Stack sugar cubes using icing as mortar to make the chimney foundation. Pipe icing on the flat side of cocoa-dusted nuts or candies that resemble large rocks. Begin at the chimney base and attach the nuts or candies to the sugar cubes. If your house is a formal style, line the nuts up; for a more casual style, apply them randomly as shown here.

hold the cone with a wooden skewer so you don't touch the icing

if you use a plastic coupler, you can switch decorating nozzles while using the same piping bag

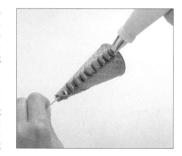

STEP 10

Decorating the Trees

Tint extra icing with green food coloring. Pipe onto ice cream cones with a leaf nozzle. Decorate as desired with candies, sprinkles, or a different color icing to make a garland.

To finish the cottage, ice the surface of the base board, and use a metal icing spatula or the back of a spoon to texture the icing into decorative swirls and ridges. Place trees in the icing and, if desired, create a path to the front door with peppermints. Pipe icing onto the roof edge to create icicles and dust the roof with confectioners sugar. Cookie "children" play in the front garden; to make them, use the recipe for Holiday Cookies on page 160.

For a summer cottage, add a few drops of green food coloring to the icing to create "grass", and arrange colorful candies over it to represent flowers.

Decorative cutouts reveal a filling of raspberry jam that glistens like stained glass. A sprinkling of confectioners sugar creates a delicate frame.

Linzer Sandwich Rings

The combination of a ground almond pastry and raspberry jam is the basis
for Linzertorte, a large version of these little cookies. Experiment with
other types of jam and other nuts for the dough.

INGREDIENTS

3/4 cup/6 oz/180 g butter
or margarine, softened

2/3 cup/5 oz/155 g packed
brown sugar

1 1/2 teaspoons baking powder

1 teaspoon finely shredded
lemon peel

1 teaspoon ground cinnamon

1/4 teaspoon ground allspice

1/4 teaspoon salt

2 egg yolks

1 teaspoon vanilla extract

2 cups/8 oz/250 g all-purpose
(plain) flour

1 cup/4 oz/125 g ground walnuts
or almonds

confectioners (icing) sugar

1/4 cup/2 fl oz/60 ml seedless
raspberry jam

Preparation Time 40 minutes
Chilling Time 1 hour
Baking Time 7 to 9 minutes
Makes about 36 cookies

METHOD FOR MAKING LINZER SANDWICH RINGS

In a large mixing bowl beat the butter or margarine with an electric mixer on medium to high speed for 30 seconds. Add the brown sugar, baking powder, lemon peel, cinnamon, allspice, and salt and beat till combined. Beat in the egg yolks and vanilla. Beat in as much of the flour as you can with the mixer. Stir in any remaining flour and ground walnuts or almonds with a wooden spoon. Divide dough in half. Cover and chill for 1 hour, or till dough is easy to handle.

On a lightly floured surface, roll each half of dough to a 1/8-in/3-mm thickness. Using a 2- or 2 1/2-in/5- or 6-cm scalloped round, star-, or heart-shaped biscuit cutter, cut out dough. Place 1 in/2.5 cm apart on ungreased baking sheets. Using a 1-in/2.5-cm cutter, cut out the centers of half the unbaked cookies. Remove the centers and reroll dough.

Bake cookies in a preheated 375°F/190°C/Gas Mark 4 oven for 7 to 9 minutes, or till edges are firm and bottoms are browned. Remove cookies with a spatula and cool on a rack.

To assemble cookie sandwiches, sift confectioners sugar over the tops of the cookies with cutouts in centers. Set aside. Spread about 1/2 teaspoon of the jam onto the bottom of each cookie without a cutout; top with a cutout cookie, confectioners sugar–side up. (Store cookies unassembled, without confectioners sugar and jam, then assemble them up to several hours before serving.)

Per cookie 107 calories/449 kilojoules, 1 g protein, 12 g carbohydrate, 6 g total fat (3 g saturated), 22 mg cholesterol, 64 mg sodium, 43 mg potassium

STEP 1

Hollowing Centers

Transfer the dough rounds to ungreased baking sheets; arrange them 1 in/2.5 cm apart. Cut out the center of half of the unbaked cookies with a 1-in/2.5-cm cutter.

STEPS FOR MAKING SANDWICH RINGS

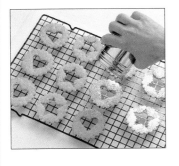

STEP 2

Sprinkling Sugar

Sift confectioners sugar over the tops of the baked and cooled cutout cookies only. Use a confectioners sugar sifter with a mesh cover, or a wire sieve.

STEP 3

Assembling Rings

Spread a thin layer of raspberry jam on the flat side of each bottom cookie. Set a cutout cookie over the jam to make a "sandwich."

About Walnuts

Sometimes called English walnuts, these slightly floury nuts, with their intricately carved appearance, often feature as a garnish on cookies (usually as half a walnut), but they can also be used chopped or ground. They are most famously used in brownies, their assertive taste having a natural affinity with chocolate. Walnuts have a stronger flavor than almonds, and when finely chopped or ground, they have a chewy texture. When buying them in their shell, look for the smallest examples, these usually have the most flavor; and make sure the two halves of the shell are tightly closed. Shelled walnuts don't keep very well, and go rancid rather quickly. If you've had shelled walnuts for some time, taste one before using in your cookie recipe and throw them out if they're soft and shrivelled or show any signs of mold. Store them in an airtight container in the refrigerator for no more than three months.

The skin of walnuts is slightly bitter and should be removed before the nuts are used in any really delicate dish. Walnuts are peeled by toasting and sifting (see pages 20 and 21) or, if you don't want to toast them first, place the nuts in a bowl and pour boiling water over them. Leave for a few minutes, drain, and, as soon as the nuts are cool enough to handle, remove the skin with your fingers. You won't get all the skin off: walnuts have too many nooks and crannies for that.

Honey Snowflakes

**For this unusual recipe, the "frosting" cooks together with the cookie.
Don't worry about making too many; they store beautifully.**

INGREDIENTS

COOKIES

1/2 cup/4 oz/125 g butter or margarine, softened

1/2 cup/3 1/2 oz/105 g packed brown sugar

1 teaspoon baking powder

1/2 teaspoon ground cardamom

1 egg

1/2 cup/6 fl oz/185 ml honey

2 cups/8 oz/250 g all-purpose (plain) flour

1 cup/4 oz/125 g wholemeal flour

FROSTING

1/4 cup/2 oz/60 g butter or margarine, softened

1/4 cup/1 oz/30 g all-purpose (plain) flour

2 teaspoons water

Preparation Time 25 minutes
Chilling Time 3 hours
Baking Time 7 to 9 minutes
Makes 4 to 5 dozen cookies

Like real alpine snowflakes, no two of these iced, honey-and-spice-scented cookie stars are exactly alike.

METHOD FOR MAKING HONEY SNOWFLAKES

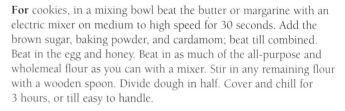

For cookies, in a mixing bowl beat the butter or margarine with an electric mixer on medium to high speed for 30 seconds. Add the brown sugar, baking powder, and cardamom; beat till combined. Beat in the egg and honey. Beat in as much of the all-purpose and wholemeal flour as you can with a mixer. Stir in any remaining flour with a wooden spoon. Divide dough in half. Cover and chill for 3 hours, or till easy to handle.

For frosting, in a mixing bowl stir together the butter or margarine, flour, and water till smooth.

On a lightly floured surface, roll each half of dough to a ¼-in/6-mm thickness. Using a 2- or 2½-in/5- or 6-cm 6-pointed star or scalloped round cutter, cut dough into shapes. Place cookies 2 in/5 cm apart on ungreased baking sheets. Pipe frosting on unbaked cookies with a piping bag and writing nozzle.

Bake cookies in a preheated 375°F/190°C/Gas Mark 4 oven for 7 to 9 minutes, or till edges are firm and bottoms are lightly browned. Remove cookies and cool on a rack.

Per cookie 75 calories/315 kilojoules, 1 g protein, 11 g carbohydrate, 3 g total fat (2 g saturated), 12 mg cholesterol, 36 mg sodium, 28 mg potassium

STEP 1

Filling Piping Bag
Fit a piping bag with a plain writing nozzle. Fold back the top of the bag to form a collar; slip one hand under the collar to steady the bag. With a rubber spatula, fill bag with frosting. Twist top of bag above frosting to close. Squeeze out some frosting to eliminate air bubbles.

STEP 2

Piping Frosting
Arrange the cookies 2 in/5 cm apart on ungreased baking sheets. Pipe the frosting in delicate patterns on each cookie, squeezing the bag with steady, even pressure. Vary the pattern from cookie to cookie.

Sophisticated cookie pinwheels seem to be in motion even when resting on a plate. Glossy fruit jam and a delicate sprinkle of chopped nuts dot the center of each.

154

Cutout Cookies

Raspberry Pinwheels

This cookie dough is sturdy enough to withstand cutting and shaping, yet it remains rich and tasty. Serve these beauties at your next party.

INGREDIENTS

1/3 cup/3 oz/90 g butter or margarine, softened

1/3 cup/3 oz/90 g cream cheese, softened

2/3 cup/5 oz/155 g granulated sugar

1 teaspoon baking powder

1 egg

1 teaspoon vanilla extract

2 cups/8 oz/250 g all-purpose (plain) flour

1/3 cup/3 fl oz/80 ml seedless raspberry, strawberry, or apricot jam

1/4 cup/1 1/2 oz/45 g finely chopped pistachio nuts or almonds

Preparation Time 30 minutes
Chilling Time 3 hours
Baking Time 8 to 10 minutes
Makes about 32 cookies

155

METHOD FOR MAKING RASPBERRY PINWHEELS

In a mixing bowl beat the butter or margarine and cream cheese with an electric mixer on medium to high speed for 30 seconds. Add the sugar and baking powder; beat till combined. Beat in the egg and vanilla. Beat in as much of the flour as you can with the mixer. Stir in any remaining flour with a wooden spoon. Divide dough in half. Cover and chill for about 3 hours, or till it is easy to handle.

On a lightly floured surface, roll each half of the dough to a 10-in/25-cm square. Using a pastry wheel or sharp knife, cut each square into sixteen 2½-in/6-cm squares. Place ½ inch apart on ungreased baking sheets. Use a knife to cut 1-in/2.5-cm slits from each corner to center. Drop ½ teaspoon of the jam in each center. Fold every other tip to the center to form a pinwheel. Sprinkle chopped nuts in the center and press firmly to seal.

Bake in a preheated 350°F/180°C/Gas Mark 4 oven for 8 to 10 minutes, or till edges are firm and lightly browned. Cool on baking sheets for 1 minute. Remove cookies and cool on a rack.

Per cookie 86 calories/361 kilojoules, 1 g protein, 12 g carbohydrate, 4 g total fat (2 g saturated), 15 mg cholesterol, 33 mg sodium, 27 mg potassium

STEP 1

Cutting Squares

On a lightly floured surface, roll out each half of chilled dough to a 10-in/25-cm square (trim to exact dimensions). With a plain or fluted pastry wheel, cut each into sixteen 2¹/₂-in/6-cm squares.

STEP 2

Cutting Slits

Transfer the squares to ungreased baking sheets. Use a sharp knife to cut 1-in/2.5-cm slits from each corner to the center. If needed, dip the knife blade in flour to keep the dough from sticking to it.

STEP 3

Shaping Cookies

Place 1/2 teaspoon of the jam in the center of each cookie. Fold over every other tip to the center to form the pinwheel. The dough will stick to the jam. Sprinkle with chopped nuts.

About Jam

Jam (or jelly) is a classic way to sandwich together two cookies. Sometimes a spoonful is placed on top of a cookie before it is baked, or the jam can fill an indentation in a just-baked cookie. A more unusual use for jam in cookies is to add it to the uncooked batter to enrich it (see Chocolate-Raspberry Brownies on page 92).

The jam most often used in cookies is raspberry – apart from having a special affinity with chocolate mixtures, raspberry jam has just enough tartness to give sweet cookies a touch of sophistication. Plum jam is also a favorite. When choosing jams, go for the best brands with lots of fruit and not too much sugar. When you've gone to the trouble to make your own cookies, why spoil them with cheap jam? Most jams used in cookie making are seedless jams or jellies. If you can't find a seedless jam you like, buy a good quality jam or preserve, heat it gently and strain it through a fine sieve before using.

Holiday Cookies

**Children will have a great time helping decorate the myriad shapes
that can be cut from this basic cookie dough.**

INGREDIENTS

COOKIES

1/3 cup/3 oz/90 g solid vegetable
shortening

1/3 cup/3 oz/90 g butter or
margarine, softened

3/4 cup/6 oz/185 g granulated
sugar

1 teaspoon baking powder

1/4 teaspoon salt

1 egg

1 tablespoon milk

1 teaspoon vanilla extract

2 cups/8 oz/250 g all-purpose
(plain) flour

ICING

1 cup/4 oz/125 g sifted
confectioners (icing) sugar

1/4 teaspoon vanilla extract

1 tablespoon milk

few drops food coloring
(optional)

Eat your way through the holiday calendar by making buttery sugar-cookie shapes for every festive occasion. Tinted icing gives them extra personality.

METHOD FOR MAKING HOLIDAY COOKIES

Preparation Time 30 minutes
Chilling Time 3 hours
Baking Time 7 to 8 minutes
Makes 36 to 48 cookies

For cookies, in a large mixing bowl beat the shortening and butter or margarine with an electric mixer on medium to high speed for 30 seconds. Add the sugar, baking powder, and salt; beat till combined. Beat in the egg, milk, and vanilla. Beat in as much of the flour as you can with the mixer. Stir in any remaining flour with a wooden spoon. Divide dough in half. Cover and chill for 3 hours, or till dough is easy to handle.

On a lightly floured surface, roll each half of the dough to an 1/8-in/3-mm thickness. Using 2- or 2 1/2-in/5- or 6-cm cutters, cut dough into desired holiday shapes, such as hearts, shamrocks, eggs, rabbits, flags, angels, or stars. Place 1 in/ 2.5 cm apart on ungreased baking sheets.

Bake in a preheated 375°F/190°C/Gas Mark 4 oven for 7 to 8 minutes, or till edges are firm and bottoms are lightly

browned. Remove cookies and cool on a rack.

Meanwhile, for icing, in a small mixing bowl stir together confectioners sugar, vanilla, and enough of the milk to make an icing of piping consistency. If desired, stir in food coloring. Use a piping bag and writing nozzle to decorate cookies with icing.

Per cookie 95 calories/399 kilojoules, 1 g protein, 15 g carbohydrate, 4 g total fat (2 g saturated), 11 mg cholesterol, 39 mg sodium, 12 mg potassium

Chocolate-Cherry Parson's Hats

You can use green maraschino cherries, pieces of other kinds of candied fruit, or different flavors of jam to make infinite variations on this recipe.

INGREDIENTS

³/₄ cup/6 oz/185 g butter or margarine, softened

³/₄ cup/6 oz/185 g granulated sugar

¹/₃ cup/1 oz/30 g unsweetened cocoa powder

¹/₂ teaspoon baking powder

1 egg

¹/₄ teaspoon almond extract

1³/₄ cups/7 oz/220 g all-purpose (plain) flour

30 maraschino cherries or ¹/₂ cup/ 4 fl oz/125 ml cherry jam

1¹/₂ oz/45 g white chocolate

1 teaspoon solid vegetable shortening

Preparation Time 25 minutes
Chilling Time 3 hours
Baking Time 10 to 12 minutes
Makes about 30 cookies

*A sweet maraschino cherry
peeps out of each icing-drizzled
chocolate triangle.*

METHOD FOR MAKING CHOCOLATE-CHERRY PARSON'S HATS

In a mixing bowl beat the butter or margarine with an electric mixer on medium to high speed for 30 seconds. Add the sugar, cocoa powder, and baking powder; beat till combined. Beat in the egg and almond extract. Beat in as much of the flour as you can with the mixer. Stir in any remaining flour with a wooden spoon. Cover and chill for 3 hours, or till dough is easy to handle.

On a lightly floured surface, roll dough to a 1/4-in/6-mm thickness. Using a 2 1/2-in/6-cm round cutter, cut dough into rounds. Place a maraschino cherry or 1 teaspoon of the cherry jam onto the center of each round.

To form each three-cornered hat, lift up 3 edges of each dough round. Fold the edges toward, but not over, the filling. Then pinch the 3 outer points together. Place cookies 2 in/5 cm apart on ungreased baking sheets.

Bake in a preheated 350°F/180°C/Gas Mark 4 oven for 10 to 12 minutes, or till edges are firm. Remove cookies and cool on a rack.

In a small, heavy saucepan, melt white chocolate and shortening over low heat; drizzle over cookies.

Per cookie 196 calories/823 kilojoules, 21 g protein, 18 g carbohydrate, 4 g fat (1 g saturated), 69 mg cholesterol, 311 mg sodium, 286 mg potassium

Cutout Cookies

Molasses & Ginger Stars

These spicy, crisp cookies are perfect for autumn picnics.
Look for candied ginger among the other spices at
your supermarket, or at gourmet food shops.

INGREDIENTS

DOUGH

1 cup/8 oz/250 g butter or margarine, softened

2/3 cup/5 oz/155 g packed brown sugar

1 tablespoon very finely chopped candied (crystallized) ginger or 1 teaspoon ground ginger

1/2 teaspoon baking soda

1/2 cup/4 fl oz/125 ml molasses or golden syrup

1/3 cup/3 fl oz/80 ml milk

3 1/2 cups/14 oz/440 g all-purpose (plain) flour

ICING

3 cups/12 oz/375 g confectioners (icing) sugar

2 to 3 tablespoons milk

Preparation Time 25 minutes
Chilling Time 3 hours
Baking Time 7 to 9 minutes
Makes about 60 cookies

Little stars flavored with molasses and candied ginger taste like crisp gingerbread, a classic holiday cookie.

METHOD FOR MAKING MOLASSES & GINGER STARS

For dough, in a large mixing bowl beat butter or margarine with an electric mixer on medium to high speed for 30 seconds. Add the brown sugar, candied or ground ginger, and baking soda; beat till combined. Beat in molasses or golden syrup and milk. Beat in as much of the flour as you can with the mixer. Stir in any remaining flour with a wooden spoon. Divide dough in half. Cover and chill for 3 hours, or till easy to handle.

On a lightly floured surface, roll each half of dough to a 1/4-in/6-mm thickness. Using a 2-in/5-cm star cutter, cut dough into star shapes. Place cookies 1 in/2.5 cm apart on greased baking sheets.

Bake in a preheated 375°F/190°C/Gas Mark 4 oven for about 7 to 9 minutes, or till edges are firm. Remove cookies and cool on a rack.

Meanwhile, for icing, in a medium mixing bowl stir together the confectioners sugar and enough of the milk to make an icing of drizzling consistency. Drizzle icing over cookies.

Per cookie 89 calories/373 kilojoules, 1 g protein, 15 g carbohydrate, 3 g total fat (2 g saturated), 8 mg cholesterol, 45 mg sodium, 45 mg potassium

Meringue-topped Lemon Thins

The meringue on these dainty, wafer-like cookies makes a wonderfully chewy and festive topping.

INGREDIENTS

1 cup/8 oz/250 g butter
or margarine, softened

1/2 cup/4 oz/125 g granulated
sugar

1 tablespoon finely shredded
lemon peel

1/4 teaspoon baking powder

1/4 teaspoon salt

1/4 teaspoon lemon extract

2 cups/8 oz/250 g all-purpose
(plain) flour

2 egg whites

2/3 cup/5 oz/155 g
granulated sugar

1/2 cup/2 oz/60 g flaked
almonds

Preparation Time 30 minutes
Chilling Time 3 hours
Baking Time 11 minutes
Makes about 42 cookies

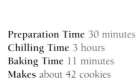

Sophisticated meringue and flaked almonds top delicate, meltingly tender lemon crescents.

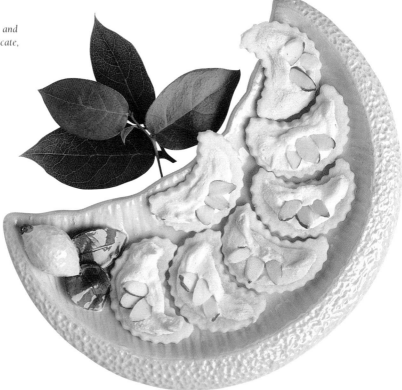

METHOD FOR MAKING MERINGUE-TOPPED LEMON THINS

In a large mixing bowl beat butter or margarine with an electric mixer on medium to high speed for 30 seconds. Add ½ cup/4 oz/ 125 g sugar, lemon peel, baking powder and salt; beat till combined. Beat in lemon extract. Beat in as much of the flour as you can with the mixer. Stir in remaining flour with a wooden spoon. Divide dough in half, cover and chill for about 3 hours, or till easy to handle.

On a lightly floured surface, roll each half of dough to a ¼-in/6-mm thickness. Cut into desired shapes using 2- or 2½-in/5- or 6-cm cookie cutters. Place 1 in/2.5 cm apart on ungreased baking sheets.

In another mixing bowl beat the egg whites with an electric mixer till soft peaks form. Gradually beat in the ⅔ cup/5 oz/155 g sugar till stiff peaks form. Spread 1 rounded teaspoon over each cookie; sprinkle a few flaked almonds over each cookie. (Chill egg white mixture between batches.)

Bake in a preheated 350°F/180°C/Gas Mark 4 oven for about 11 minutes, or till meringue is lightly browned. Remove cookies and cool on a rack.

Per cookie 90 calories/378 kilojoules, 1 g protein, 10 g carbohydrate, 5 g total fat (3 g saturated), 12 mg cholesterol, 68 mg sodium, 22 mg potassium

Cutout Cookies

Fruity Foldovers

Soft, fruit-filled cookies are loved by both children and adults. Here's an easy version that will please the whole family. The cookies store well in an airtight container at room temperature or in the freezer.

INGREDIENTS

1/2 cup/4 oz/125 g butter or margarine, softened

1/4 cup/2 oz/60 g packed brown sugar

1/2 teaspoon baking soda

1/2 teaspoon ground coriander

1/4 teaspoon salt

1 egg

1/2 cup/4 fl oz/125 ml honey

1 teaspoon vanilla extract

2 1/2 cups/10 oz/315 g all-purpose (plain) flour

1/3 cup/3 fl oz/80 ml apple or red currant jelly

1 cup/6 oz/185 g chopped mixed dried fruits (such as apricots, apples, peaches, prunes, dates, or raisins)

1/2 cup/2 oz/60 g finely chopped pecans or walnuts

sifted confectioners (icing) sugar

*Sugar-dusted cookie
turnovers filled with
a harvest of dried fruits
and nuts can also be served
hot with ice cream.*

METHOD FOR MAKING FRUITY FOLDOVERS

Preparation Time 40 minutes
Chilling Time 3 hours
Baking Time 7 to 9 minutes
Makes about 50 cookies

STEPS AT A GLANCE	Page
Making cookie dough	12–17
Chopping fruit	49
Making cutout cookies	126–131

In a mixing bowl beat butter or margarine with an electric mixer on medium to high speed for 30 seconds. Add brown sugar, baking soda, coriander, and salt; beat till combined. Beat in the egg, honey, and vanilla. Beat in as much of the flour as you can with the mixer. Stir in any remaining flour with a wooden spoon. Divide dough in half. Cover and chill for 3 hours, or till dough is easy to handle.

Meanwhile, in a small saucepan heat apple or red currant jelly till melted. Remove from heat. Stir in the dried fruit and pecans or walnuts.

On a lightly floured surface roll each half of the dough to a 1/8-in/3-mm thickness. Using a 2 1/2-in/6-cm round cookie cutter, cut into rounds. Place cookies 1/2 in/12 mm apart on ungreased baking sheets.

Spoon 1 teaspoon of the dried fruit mixture onto the center of each round. Fold half of the round over the filling, creating a half-moon shape. Seal cut edges of each round with the tines of a fork.

Bake in a preheated 375°F/190°C/Gas Mark 4 oven for 7 to 9 minutes, or till bottoms are lightly browned. Remove cookies and cool on a rack. Sprinkle lightly with confectioners sugar.

Per cookie 72 calories/302 kilojoules, 1 g protein, 12 g carbohydrate, 3 g total fat (1 g saturated), 9 mg cholesterol, 44 mg sodium, 38 mg potassium

About Pecans

Native to America and harvested in the autumn, pecans are similar in appearance and taste to walnuts, but oilier. Shelled pecans will become rancid more quickly than most other nuts. If buying them shelled, purchase small quantities as you need them, and store leftover nuts in an airtight container in the refrigerator.

Unshelled nuts should have smooth, unblemished, uncracked shells. If, when you shake the nut, the kernel rattles, discard it; it means the kernel is old and has shrivelled. Like walnuts, shelled pecans are hard to peel because of their knobbly appearance. Toast and sift them (as shown on pages 20 and 21) or pour boiling water over untoasted nuts, leave for a few minutes, drain and then peel with the fingers. Do not be concerned if all the skin doesn't come off. When a recipe asks for finely chopped pecans, don't bother to peel them.

Pecans are used whole, as a garnish (sometimes candied), chopped or ground. They go particularly well with maple syrup and honey—Pecan Pie is the best evidence of that—and are often used in sticky toppings (see Coffee-Pecan Triangles on page 112).

SLICED COOKIES

BASIC TOOLS FOR MAKING SLICED COOKIES

For sliced cookies, it's best to chill the log of dough in a tall glass and store on its side so the dough won't flatten, then when firm, cut it into rounds with a sharp knife and bake on a baking sheet. Use a spatula to transfer the finished cookies to a wire cooling rack.

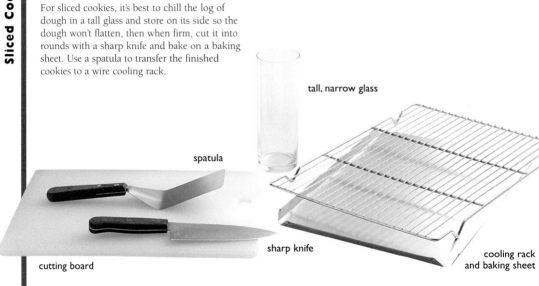

tall, narrow glass

spatula

sharp knife

cutting board

cooling rack
and baking sheet

Making Sliced Cookies

Sliced cookies, also called refrigerator cookies and icebox cookies, are the ultimate in convenience. You make the dough when you have the time, roll it into a log, wrap in plastic and store in the refrigerator for up to 1 week, or the freezer for up to 1 month. When you want cookies in a hurry all you have to do is slice them and bake them. You don't even have to use the whole log at once—just cut off what you need and return the rest to the refrigerator or freezer. Very cold dough cuts into thin slices more easily, so you get the added advantage of being able to make thin wafer cookies in no time at all.

When unexpected guests arrive, when your child brings home a friend from school, or when you've run out of ideas for dessert, you can remove your ready-made log of cookie dough from the fridge or freezer and slice your way out of trouble.

Sliced cookie dough is too soft to cut initially, very like the mixture used for cutout cookies. The two doughs are similar in their early stages—both have similar consistencies and are refrigerated—but differ in how

MAKING SLICED COOKIES

they are shaped. While cutouts are punched out of a rolled dough sheet, sliced cookies are cut from a solid dough log. To add texture and flavor, some doughs are rolled in chopped nuts, like Chocolate-Pistachio Sandwich Cookies (page 188), or tinted with chocolate, sliced, and reassembled into two-color checkerboards like those on page 184 or stacked into stripes like the Chocolate-Peppermint Slices on page 199. A nicely rounded shape is an important part of the visual appeal of sliced cookies, especially when they're sandwiched together like these Marshmallow Sandwich Cookies (page 205). If the dough flattens as you slice it, roll it back into a log and chill it again for 5 to 10 minutes.

plastic wrap keeps
the dough from
sticking to your
fingers

STEP 1

Shaping Dough

Divide the dough in half. Place each half on a sheet of plastic wrap large enough to fully enclose it. Roll the dough into a log inside the wrap. Seal the ends airtight.

lay the glass on
its side in the
refrigerator

STEP 2

Storing Log of Dough

To keep the log nicely rounded, chill it inside a tall, narrow glass (if the log is longer than your glass, cut it into several portions and store it in several glasses). Alternatively, just chill the dough wrapped in plastic.

chill the dough log briefly if it softens and loses its shape when you slice it

STEP 3

Slicing Cookies

Unwrap the chilled log of dough. Cut it into
1/4-in/6-mm-thick slices with a sharp knife. Always use a
knife with a thin, sharp blade and slice with a back-and-
forth sawing motion, not a downward swipe.

for cookies made with a lot of spices or with chocolate, look for firm edges and a dull surface to indicate doneness

STEP 4

Testing for Doneness

Bake in a preheated 375°F/190°C/Gas Mark 4 oven until
the edges are firm and the bottoms are lightly browned,
8 to 10 minutes, or as the recipe directs. Remove from
the baking sheet to a wire rack to cool completely.

Although they look plain, these simple sliced cookies are full of flavor. Sugar-topped Rum & Spice Cookies are on page 192.

Simple two-tone checkerboards are very impressive. They look marvellous and taste as good as they look.

Chocolate & Vanilla Checkerboards

So easy, yet so dramatic. And you don't really need to tell anyone how simple these checkerboard cookies are to make. If pressed for time, make and assemble the spliced logs, then chill until the next day when all you need to do is to slice and bake them.

INGREDIENTS

1 cup/8 oz/250 g butter or margarine, softened

1/2 cup/4 oz/125 g granulated sugar

1/2 cup/3 1/2 oz/105 g packed brown sugar

1 1/2 teaspoons baking powder

1 egg

2 teaspoons vanilla extract

3 1/4 cups/13 oz/400 g all-purpose (plain) flour

1/3 cup/2 oz/60 g unsweetened (bitter) chocolate, melted and cooled

Preparation Time 45 minutes
Chilling Time 2 hours
Baking Time 8 to 10 minutes
Makes about 64 cookies

STEPS AT A GLANCE	Page
Making cookie dough	12–17
Melting chocolate	20

METHOD FOR MAKING CHOCOLATE & VANILLA CHECKERBOARDS

In a large mixing bowl beat the butter or margarine with an electric mixer on medium to high speed for 30 seconds. Add the granulated sugar, brown sugar, and baking powder; beat till combined. Beat in the egg and vanilla. Beat in as much of the flour as you can with the mixer. Stir in any remaining flour with a wooden spoon. Divide dough in half.

Knead melted chocolate into half of dough till combined. Shape plain and chocolate halves of dough into 8-in/20-cm logs. Wrap each in waxed paper or plastic wrap. Chill for 2 hours, or till firm. Cut each chilled log lengthwise into quarters; reassemble logs, alternating chocolate and vanilla quarters. Wrap and refrigerate for 15 to 30 minutes, or till well chilled.

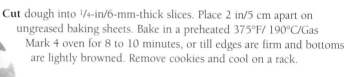

Cut dough into 1/4-in/6-mm-thick slices. Place 2 in/5 cm apart on ungreased baking sheets. Bake in a preheated 375°F/ 190°C/Gas Mark 4 oven for 8 to 10 minutes, or till edges are firm and bottoms are lightly browned. Remove cookies and cool on a rack.

Per cookie 65 calories/273 kilojoules, 1 g protein, 8 g carbohydrate, 3 g total fat (2 g saturated), 11 mg cholesterol, 36 mg sodium, 22 mg potassium

STEP 1

Adding Chocolate
Divide the dough into 2 equal pieces. Knead the melted chocolate into 1 piece of dough until completely blended without any streaks remaining.

STEP 2

Cutting Dough
Be sure the dough is thoroughly chilled. Cut each chocolate and vanilla log into quarters with a knife that is very sharp and has a long, thin blade.

STEP 3

Reassembling Logs
Press together 1 chocolate piece and 1 vanilla piece to form a half moon. Set another chocolate piece on top of the vanilla. Insert a vanilla piece next to it. You should now have a whole log with alternating chocolate and vanilla quarters. Wrap tightly and chill.

Chocolate-Pistachio Sandwich Cookie

Some gourmet or natural food shops carry shelled pistachios in bulk,
which makes cooking with them cheaper and easier on the fingers
than having to shell them at home.

INGREDIENTS

COOKIES

1 cup/8 oz/250 g butter or margarine, softened

1 cup/8 oz/250 g granulated sugar

1/2 cup/3 1/2 oz/105 g packed brown sugar

1/3 cup/1 oz/30 g unsweetened cocoa powder

1 teaspoon baking powder

1/4 teaspoon ground nutmeg

1 egg

1 1/2 teaspoons vanilla extract

2 cups/8 oz/250 g all-purpose (plain) flour

2/3 cup/4 oz/125 g ground pistachios, almonds, or pecans

FILLING

1/4 cup/3 tablespoons butter or margarine, softened

1/4 cup/3/4 oz/20 g unsweetened cocoa powder

2 cups/8 oz/250 g sifted confectioners (icing) sugar

2 tablespoons milk

3/4 teaspoon vanilla extract

extra milk (if required)

Pale green pistachio nuts form a halo of color and texture on the edges of chocolate sandwiches filled with an enticing milk-chocolate butter cream.

METHOD FOR MAKING CHOCOLATE-PISTACHIO SANDWICH COOKIES

Preparation Time 45 minutes
Chilling Time 2 hours
Baking Time 8 to 10 minutes
Makes about 32 cookies

STEPS AT A GLANCE	Page
Making cookie dough	**12–17**
Grinding nuts	**45**

For cookies, in a large mixing bowl beat the butter or margarine with an electric mixer on medium to high speed for 30 seconds. Add the granulated sugar, brown sugar, cocoa powder, baking powder, and nutmeg; beat till combined. Beat in the egg and vanilla. Beat in as much of the flour as you can with the mixer. Stir in any remaining flour with a wooden spoon. Divide dough in half. Cover and chill for 30 minutes, or till dough can be shaped into rolls. Shape dough into two 8-in/20-cm rolls. Roll in ground pistachios, almonds, or pecans to coat. Wrap in waxed paper or plastic wrap. Chill dough for 2 hours, or till firm.

For filling, in a bowl beat butter or margarine till fluffy. Beat in cocoa powder. Gradually add 1 cup (about 5 oz/155 g) of the confectioners sugar, beating well. Slowly beat in the milk and vanilla. Gradually beat in the remaining confectioners sugar. Beat in additional milk, if needed, to make a mixture of spreading consistency.

Cut dough into 1/4-in/6-mm-thick slices. Place 2 in/5 cm apart on ungreased baking sheets. Bake in a preheated 375°F/ 190°C/Gas Mark 4 oven for 8 to 10 minutes, or till edges are firm. Remove cookies and cool on a rack.

Spread 1 to 2 teaspoons of the filling over the bottoms of half the cookies; top with remaining cookies, bottom sides down.

Per cookie 174 calories/730 kilojoules, 2 g protein, 23 g carbohydrate, 9 g total fat (4 g saturated), 25 mg cholesterol, 83 mg sodium, 57 mg potassium

STEP 1

Coating with Nuts

Arrange the ground nuts in an 8-in/ 20-cm square on a sheet of waxed paper. Gently roll a log of chocolate cookie dough across the nuts.

STEP 2

Making Filling

Gradually beat the confectioners sugar and milk in small amounts into the cocoa-butter mixture, alternating sugar and milk until the mixture is creamy and ready to spread.

Rum-flavored spice cookies glitter with a topping of sugar crystals and allspice.

Rum & Spice Cookies

Try brandy in place of the rum or, for a non-alcoholic version, substitute
3 tablespoons of water and 2 teaspoon rum extract for the rum.

INGREDIENTS

3/4 cup/6 oz/185 g butter or margarine, softened

1 cup/8 oz/250 g granulated sugar

1 teaspoon baking powder

1/2 teaspoon baking soda

1/2 teaspoon ground allspice

1 egg

1/4 cup/2 fl oz/60 ml honey

3 tablespoons rum

2 2/3 cups/11 oz/340 g all-purpose (plain) flour

1/3 cup/3 oz/90 g granulated sugar

3/4 teaspoon ground allspice

Preparation Time 30 minutes
Chilling Time 2 to 3 hours
Baking Time 8 to 10 minutes
Makes about 64 cookies

STEPS AT A GLANCE	Page
Making cookie dough	12–17
Making sliced cookies	178–183

METHOD FOR MAKING RUM & SPICE COOKIES

In a large mixing bowl beat the butter or margarine with an electric mixer on medium to high speed for 30 seconds. Add 1 cup/8 oz/250 g sugar, baking powder, baking soda, and ½ teaspoon allspice; beat till combined. Beat in the egg, honey, and rum. Beat in as much of the flour as you can with the mixer. Stir in any remaining flour with a wooden spoon. Divide dough in half. Cover and chill for 1 hour, or till dough can be shaped into rolls.

In a 9-in/23-cm pie plate, stir together ⅓ cup/3 oz/90 g sugar and ¾ teaspoon allspice. Shape each half of dough into an 8-in/20-cm roll; roll each in the sugar-allspice mixture to coat. Wrap in waxed paper or plastic wrap. Chill for 2 hours, or till firm. Cover and reserve remaining sugar and spice mixture.

Cut the chilled dough into ¼-in/6-mm-thick slices. Place slices about 2 in/5 cm apart on lightly greased baking sheets. Sprinkle with reserved sugar-allspice mixture. Bake in a preheated 375°F/190°C/Gas Mark 4 oven for 8 to 10 minutes, or till edges are firm and bottoms are lightly browned. Remove cookies and cool on a rack.

Per cookie 58 calories/243 kilojoules, 1 g protein, 9 g carbohydrate, 2 g total fat (1 g saturated), 9 mg cholesterol, 36 mg sodium, 9 mg potassium

Mocha Tea Cookies

The word mocha, which we use to mean a chocolate-coffee combination, comes from the name of a port in Yemen where coffee trees were first cultivated. Here powdered cocoa provides the chocolate flavor and instant espresso powder the coffee.

INGREDIENTS

COOKIES

3/4 cup/6 oz/185 g butter or margarine, softened

1/3 cup/2 1/2 oz/75 g packed brown sugar

1/3 cup/1 oz/30 g unsweetened cocoa powder

1 teaspoon instant espresso coffee powder

1 teaspoon vanilla extract

1/8 teaspoon salt

1 1/2 cups/6 oz/185 g all-purpose (plain) flour

ICING

3 tablespoons butter or margarine

2 1/4 cups/9 oz/280 g sifted confectioners (icing) sugar

1 teaspoon vanilla extract

1 to 2 tablespoons milk

METHOD FOR MAKING MOCHA TEA COOKIES

Preparation Time 25 minutes
Chilling Time 2 hours
Baking Time 8 to 10 minutes
Makes about 36 cookies

For cookies, in a large mixing bowl beat butter or margarine with an electric mixer on medium to high speed for 30 seconds. Add the brown sugar, cocoa powder, espresso powder, vanilla, and salt; beat till combined. Beat in as much of the flour as you can with the mixer. Stir in any remaining flour with a wooden spoon. Shape dough into one 10-in/25-cm roll. Wrap in waxed paper or plastic wrap. Chill dough for 2 hours, or till firm.

Cut dough into ¼-in/6-mm-thick slices. Place about 2 in/5 cm apart on lightly greased baking sheets. Bake in a preheated 375°F/190°C/Gas Mark 4 oven for 8 to 10 minutes, or till edges are firm and bottoms are lightly browned. Remove cookies and cool on a rack.

Meanwhile, for icing, in a medium saucepan melt butter or margarine and stir over medium heat till butter browns. Remove from heat; stir in confectioners sugar, vanilla, and enough of the milk to make an icing of spreading consistency. If icing becomes too stiff, add hot water, a few drops at a time, and stir till smooth.

Per cookie 94 calories/395 kilojoules, 1 g protein, 13 g carbohydrate, 5 g total fat
(2 g saturated), 10 mg cholesterol, 60 mg sodium, 19 mg potassium

A crown of white icing tops these
mocha-flavored cookie slices.

About Teatime

An English institution now in decline, teatime was traditionally served at 4 o'clock. There were always thin slices of bread and butter and a pot of jam, or thin sandwiches (often cucumber); anything made with bread was always to be eaten first. In winter, scones often replaced the sandwiches. Then followed cake, usually only one, unless it was a large party, and if cookies (biscuits) were served they were homemade; it was shameful to offer store-bought cookies at tea. Tea was drunk at teatime, never coffee.

To make tea, the kettle is boiled, the teapot is warmed with hot water, a teaspoon of tea is added to the pot for each person, plus an extra one "for the pot". The teapot is covered with a tea cosy and left to "draw" for a few minutes, then the tea is poured into warmed china cups through a tea strainer, and milk, sugar, and lemon slices are passed around separately.

Chocolate-Peppermint Slices

If everyone is tired of plain old sugar cookies, make this delightful variation instead.
You can make the peppermint dough any color you like just by adding
a few drops of food coloring.

INGREDIENTS

1/2 cup/4 oz/125 g butter
or margarine

1/3 cup/3 oz/90 g granulated
sugar

1/4 teaspoon baking powder

1 cup/4 oz/125 g all-purpose
(plain) flour

1 oz/30 g semisweet (plain)
chocolate, melted and cooled

1/4 teaspoon
peppermint extract

several drops food
coloring (optional)

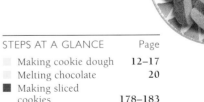

Preparation Time 35 minutes
Chilling Time 2 hours
Baking Time 8 to 10 minutes
Makes about 30 cookies

More cookie sleight of hand: simply stack two contrasting doughs, then slice and bake. The layers fuse together in the oven.

METHOD FOR MAKING CHOCOLATE-PEPPERMINT SLICES

In a medium mixing bowl beat the butter or margarine with an electric mixer on medium to high speed for 30 seconds. Add the sugar and baking powder; beat till combined. Beat in as much of the flour as you can with the mixer. Stir in any remaining flour with a wooden spoon. Divide dough in half.

Place half the dough in a small bowl. Stir in melted chocolate, then knead dough till chocolate is evenly distributed and the dough is uniformly chocolate-colored and not streaky.

Knead peppermint extract and, if desired, food coloring into remaining dough. Make sure it is well mixed into all of the dough. Shape each half of dough into a ball. Wrap in waxed paper or plastic wrap. Chill for 2 hours, or till firm. **On** a lightly floured surface, shape each half of dough into a log about 4 in/10 cm long. Roll and/or pat each log to a 6x3-in/15x7.5-cm rectangle. Cut each rectangle in half lengthwise,

forming two 6x1¹/₂-in/15x4-cm rectangles. Stack all 4 rectangles on top of each other, alternating chocolate with peppermint dough. Press down lightly. Cut the stacked layers into ¹/₄-in/6-mm-thick slices. Place slices about 1 in/2.5 cm apart on ungreased baking sheets.

Bake in a preheated 375°F/190°C/Gas Mark 4 oven for 8 to 10 minutes, or till bottoms are a light golden brown. Remove cookies and cool on a rack.

Per cookie 54 calories/226 kilojoules, 1 g protein, 6 g carbohydrate, 3 g total fat (2 g saturated), 8 mg cholesterol, 36 mg sodium, 10 mg potassium

Coconut-Orange Wafers

Two tropical flavors combine to add both taste and texture to these crisp wafers.
Serve them with ice cream.

INGREDIENTS

1/2 cup/4 oz/125 g butter or margarine, softened

1/3 cup/3 oz/90 g cream cheese, softened

1 1/2 cups/6 oz/185 g sifted confectioners (icing) sugar

1/4 teaspoon baking soda

1/4 teaspoon salt

1 egg

1 tablespoon milk

1 teaspoon finely shredded orange peel

1/4 teaspoon coconut extract

2 1/2 cups/10 oz/315 g all-purpose (plain) flour

1/2 to 3/4 cup/1 1/2 to 2 1/2 oz/ 45 to 75 g toasted shredded coconut

Preparation Time 30 minutes
Chilling Time 2 to 3 hours
Baking Time 7 to 9 minutes
Makes about 60 cookies

202

Get out the lounge chair, pour a tall glass of your favorite cool drink, then leave a plate of Coconut-Orange Wafers nearby.

METHOD FOR MAKING COCONUT-ORANGE WAFERS

In a large mixing bowl beat the butter or margarine and cream cheese with an electric mixer on medium to high speed for 30 seconds. Add the confectioners sugar, baking soda, and salt; beat till combined. Beat in the egg, milk, orange peel, and coconut extract. Beat in as much of the flour as you can with the mixer. Stir in any remaining flour with a wooden spoon. Divide dough in half. If necessary, cover and chill for 1 hour, or till dough can be shaped into rolls. Shape each half into an 8-in/20-cm roll. Roll in toasted coconut to coat all sides. Wrap each roll in waxed paper or plastic wrap. Chill for 2 hours, or till firm.

Cut dough into ¼-in/6-mm-thick slices. Place 2 in/5 cm apart on ungreased baking sheets. Bake in a preheated 375°F/190°C/Gas Mark 4 oven for 7 to 9 minutes, or till lightly browned. Remove cookies and cool on a rack.

Per cookie 50 calories/210 kilojoules, 1 g protein, 7 g carbohydrate, 2 g total fat (1 g saturated), 9 mg cholesterol, 38 mg sodium, 11 mg potassium

Marshmallow Sandwich Cookies

If marshmallow creme is unavailable, make the filling with 1⅓ cups/12 oz/375 g cream cheese, ¾ cup/3 oz/90g confectioners sugar and 1½ teaspoons vanilla extract. Stir in nuts as directed below. For personalized cookies, write initials on each in chocolate.

INGREDIENTS

COOKIES

⅓ cup/2 oz/60 g semisweet (plain) chocolate, chopped

1 cup/8 oz/250 g butter or margarine, softened

¾ cup/6 oz/185 g granulated sugar

1 teaspoon baking powder

1 egg

1 teaspoon vanilla extract

2½ cups/10 oz/315 g all-purpose (plain) flour

FILLING

⅔ cup/6 oz/185 g cream cheese, softened

1 cup/7 oz/220 g marshmallow creme

½ cup/2 oz/60 g finely chopped walnuts, pecans, or peanuts

DRIZZLE (OPTIONAL)

½ cup/3 oz/90 g semisweet (plain) chocolate or white chocolate, chopped

1 teaspoon solid vegetable shortening

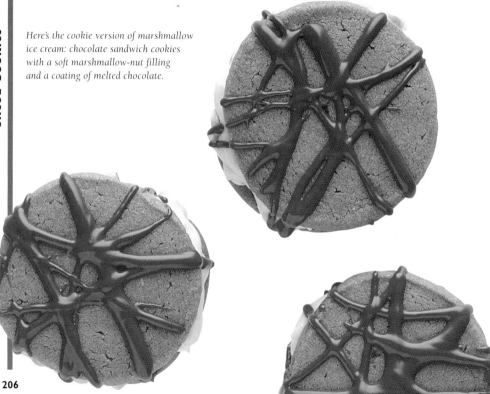

Here's the cookie version of marshmallow ice cream: chocolate sandwich cookies with a soft marshmallow-nut filling and a coating of melted chocolate.

METHOD FOR MAKING MARSHMALLOW SANDWICH COOKIES

Preparation Time 40 minutes
Chilling Time 2 hours
Baking Time 8 to 10 minutes
Makes about 32 cookies

STEPS AT A GLANCE   Page

Making cookie dough   **12–17**
Melting chocolate   **20**
Drizzling icing or chocolate   **22**

For cookies, in a small, heavy saucepan, melt chocolate over low heat, stirring constantly. Set aside. In a large mixing bowl, beat the butter or margarine with an electric mixer on medium to high speed for 30 seconds. Add the sugar and baking powder; beat till combined. Beat in the melted chocolate, egg, and vanilla. Beat in as much of the flour as you can with the mixer. Stir in any remaining flour with a wooden spoon. Shape dough into two 7-in/18-cm rolls. Wrap in waxed paper or plastic wrap. Chill dough for 2 hours, or till firm.

Cut dough into slices a little less than 1/4 in/6 mm thick. Place about 2 in/5 cm apart on un-greased baking sheets. Bake in a preheated 375°F/190°C/Gas Mark 4 oven for 8 to 10 minutes, or till edges are firm and bottoms are lightly browned. Remove cookies and cool on a rack.

Meanwhile, for filling, in a mixing bowl beat cream cheese and marshmallow creme (or ingredients for alternative filling on page 205) with an electric mixer on medium speed till blended. Stir in walnuts, pecans, or peanuts. Spread about 2 teaspoons of filling on bottoms of half of the cookies; top with remaining cookies.

If desired, for drizzle, in a small, heavy saucepan melt chocolate and shortening over low heat. Drizzle over tops of cookies. Cover and store in the refrigerator.

Per cookie 168 calories/705 kilojoules, 2 g protein, 18 g carbohydrate, 10 g total fat (7 g saturated), 28 mg cholesterol, 89 mg sodium, 46 mg potassium

SHAPED AND
MOLDED COOKIES

BASIC TOOLS FOR SHAPING AND MOLDING

Because your hands do much of the shaping, only these few tools are needed to prepare, mark, and bake cookie dough with simple designs.

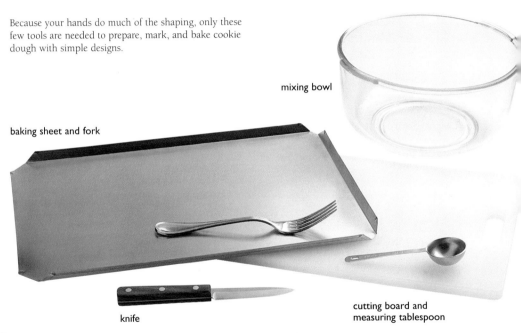

mixing bowl

baking sheet and fork

knife

cutting board and
measuring tablespoon

Shaping and Molding Cookies

Cookie dough for shaping and molding is buttery and pliable, yet more tolerant of handling than most other cookie doughs. It can be rolled, twisted, and formed into shapes, such as twisty pretzels or fluted cups, that are not possible to create with a cutter. This kind of dough also holds an impression. You can imprint it with simple linear patterns like the familiar crisscross used on Sesame Fork Cookies on page 249, or mold it to produce a cookie with a handsome rope edge and center medallion similar to Shortbread on page 222.

Shaped and molded cookies look best when all the cookies in a batch are similar in size and shape. They will also bake more evenly if each is the same size. Take a little time to become familiar with this type of dough so you can develop just the right touch for each recipe, whether it's a delicate chocolate-dipped pirouette (page 216) or a spicy coiled Cinnamon Snail (page 240). The steps for making balls and ropes from cookie dough as shown in this section demonstrate important basics that you will use throughout the chapter.

STEPS FOR SHAPING AND MOLDING COOKIES

if the balls are all
about the same
size, they will bake
in the same
amount of time

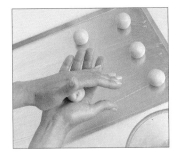

STEP 1

Shaping Balls

Divide the dough into equal portions of about
1 tablespoon each. Roll each portion between the palms
of your hands until it is nicely rounded and smooth all
over. Place the balls on lightly greased baking sheets.

chill the dough
again briefly
if the fork sticks
when you make
the pattern

STEP 2

Pressing with a Fork

Leave plenty of space between the dough balls. Flatten
the cookies with the tines of a fork, then create crisscross
lines by pressing again with the fork tines at right angles
to the first marks.

use gentle, even
pressure when
rolling so the
rope will be
uniformly thick

STEP 3

Making Ropes

Divide the dough log into ¹/₂-in/12-mm pieces.
Roll each piece into a thin 8-in/20-cm rope by working
it back and forth with your fingers on a lightly floured
surface. As you roll the dough, work from the center
out to lengthen it.

handle the rope
gently to keep its
rounded shape

STEP 4

Shaping Pretzels

Although not a true pretzel shape because it lacks the
twist shown in step 5, this shape is similar and is slightly
easier to accomplish. Lay one rope of dough on the
baking sheet. Form a circle by crossing one end over the
other, overlapping about 1 in/2.5 cm from the ends.
Bring the ends down to the opposite edge of the circle.
Press gently to seal.

Shaped and Molded Cookies

twist the dough
ends carefully
so they don't
break off

STEP 5

Shaping True Pretzels

To make a true pretzel, form a circle with a rope of
dough, crossing one end over the other about
1 in/2.5 cm from each end. Twist once where the
rope overlaps (the dough will spiral around, and the
ends of the rope will extend slightly beyond the twist).

the pressure of
your hands will
secure the dough
ends, so it isn't
necessary to
seal with water in
this case

STEP 6

Securing Twists

After the overlapped ends have been twisted once,
lift them up from the baking sheet and set them on
the opposite edge of the circle. Press down on the
ends with your fingers to attach them to the dough.

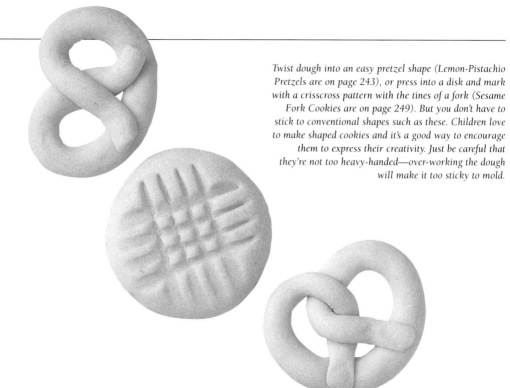

Twist dough into an easy pretzel shape (Lemon-Pistachio Pretzels are on page 243), or press into a disk and mark with a crisscross pattern with the tines of a fork (Sesame Fork Cookies are on page 249). But you don't have to stick to conventional shapes such as these. Children love to make shaped cookies and it's a good way to encourage them to express their creativity. Just be careful that they're not too heavy-handed—over-working the dough will make it too sticky to mold.

Almond Crisps

Roll these cookies around a spoon handle to make tubular pirouettes or place them on inverted muffin pans to create tulip cups. Dip pirouettes into melted chocolate, if desired. Fill cups with pudding, whipped cream, or ice cream, and fresh berries.

INGREDIENTS

2 egg whites

1/4 cup/2 oz/60 g butter
or margarine

1/2 cup/4 oz/125 g granulated
sugar

1/2 cup/2 oz/60 g all-purpose
(plain) flour

1/2 teaspoon almond extract

1/2 cup/2 1/2 oz/75 g semisweet
(plain) chocolate, chopped
(optional)

2 teaspoons solid vegetable
shortening (optional)

Preparation Time 45 minutes
Baking Time 5 to 6 minutes
Makes about 28 cookies

STEPS AT A GLANCE	Page
Melting chocolate	20
Making meringue	23

Wafer-thin cookie cups and chocolate-dipped pirouettes look professionally made, but are easy to bake at home with a light, almond-flavored batter.

METHOD FOR MAKING ALMOND CRISPS

In a medium bowl let egg whites stand for 30 minutes at room temperature. Generously grease a baking sheet. (Repeat greasing baking sheet for each batch.) Set aside. In a small saucepan heat butter or margarine over low heat just till melted. Set aside to cool.

Beat egg whites with an electric mixer on medium to high speed till soft peaks form (tips curl). Gradually add sugar, beating till stiff peaks form (tips stand straight). Fold in about half of the flour. Then gently stir in butter or margarine and almond extract. Fold in the remaining flour till combined. Drop level tablespoons of batter at least 3 in/7.5 cm apart onto prepared baking sheet. Spread batter into 3-in/7.5-cm circles. (Bake only 3 cookies at a time.) Bake in a preheated 375°F/190°C/Gas Mark 4 oven for 5 to 6 minutes, or till cookies are golden.

Immediately remove a cookie from the baking sheet. For pirouettes, place the cookie upside down on a table or benchtop and quickly roll it around the greased handle of a wooden spoon or a dowel. Slide the cookie off the handle or dowel and cool on a wire rack. Or, for tulip cups, place the warm cookie on an inverted muffin pan. Working quickly, repeat with remaining warm cookies. (If they harden before you can shape them, reheat them in the oven for about 1 minute.)

To dip pirouettes, in a small, heavy saucepan heat chocolate and shortening over low heat just till melted, stirring occasionally. Remove from heat. Dip one end of each cookie into chocolate mixture. Let excess drip off. (Or, drizzle cookies with chocolate.) Transfer to a waxed paper–lined baking sheet. Let stand till chocolate is set.

Per cookie 36 calories/151 kilojoules, 1 g protein, 5 g carbohydrate, 2 g total fat (1 g saturated), 4 mg cholesterol, 23 mg sodium, 6 mg potassium

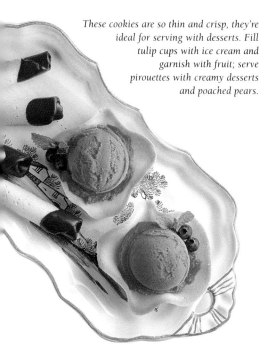

These cookies are so thin and crisp, they're ideal for serving with desserts. Fill tulip cups with ice cream and garnish with fruit; serve pirouettes with creamy desserts and poached pears.

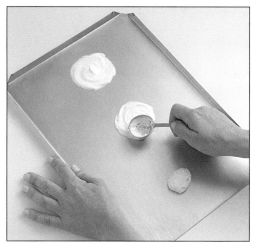

STEP 1

Spreading Batter

For each cookie, drop 1 level tablespoon of batter onto a greased baking sheet, then spread to a 3-in/7.5-cm circle with the back of a spoon.

STEP 2

Rolling Pirouettes

Place a warm cookie upside down near the edge of a benchtop or table and quickly roll it around the greased handle of a wooden spoon or a dowel. Repeat for the remaining cookies.

STEP 3

Shaping Tulip Cups

Invert a muffin pan and cover one cup with a warm cookie, pleating the cookie to form a cup. If the cookies harden before shaping, reheat them in the oven for about 1 minute.

About Almonds

Almonds are the most versatile and popular of all nuts and are available in the most forms: whole with skin, whole blanched, halved, flaked, slivered, chopped, ground, smoked, sugared, candy-coated, chocolate coated, as a paste and in almond extract. They are easy to peel—simply pour boiling water over them, wait a minute or two, drain and slip the skins off with your fingers. Toasting them adds crunch and flavor. A blanched almond placed on top of each cookie before it is baked, emerges golden and crisp from the oven, giving the cookie an extra dimension in taste.

Ground almonds can be used to replace flour in some cookie recipes, but read the label carefully if you're buying almonds ready-ground; some manufacturers add cheap fillers, and flavor the mixture with bitter almonds. If you have a food processor it is easy to grind blanched almonds yourself.

Just like any nut, almonds will become rancid if kept too long. And the more you do to them, peel, chop, flake, grind, the more quickly they will lose freshness. Buy shelled almonds in small quantities and store in an airtight container in the refrigerator for up to 3 months.

Made from a buttery dough, meltingly rich shortbread may be shaped by hand or in a decorative mold.

Shortbread

You can hardly go anywhere in Great Britain without running into this grand staple.
It is legendary in its traditional form, but we decided to come up with some
variations, too, for adventurous shortbread lovers.

INGREDIENTS

1 cup/4 oz/125 g all-purpose (plain) flour

1/3 cup/3 oz/90 g granulated sugar

1/8 teaspoon salt

1/2 cup/4 oz/125 g cold butter

1 teaspoon vanilla extract

nonstick cooking spray or vegetable oil

sifted confectioners (icing) sugar (optional)

SHORTBREAD VARIATIONS

PECAN

Stir 1/4 cup/1 oz/30 g ground
toasted pecans or walnuts into
the flour mixture.

LEMON OR ORANGE

Add 2 teaspoons finely shredded
lemon or orange peel to the
flour mixture; omit the vanilla and
add 1/4 teaspoon lemon or
orange extract.

MOCHA

Stir 2 tablespoons unsweetened
cocoa powder and 1 teaspoon
instant coffee granules into the
flour mixture

METHOD FOR MAKING SHORTBREAD

Preparation Time 15 minutes
Baking Time 25 minutes
Makes 8 or 16 wedges

STEPS AT A GLANCE   Page
■ Cutting in butter
  or margarine   84

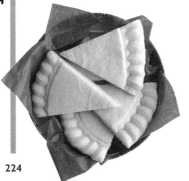

In a medium mixing bowl stir together the flour, sugar, and salt. (For shortbread variations, adjust the flour mixture as directed.) Cut in butter till mixture resembles fine crumbs. Sprinkle with vanilla. Form the mixture into a ball and knead till smooth.

Spray a wooden or ceramic shortbread mold with nonstick cooking spray or brush with oil. Firmly press the dough into the mold. Invert the mold over a lightly greased baking sheet and tap the mold lightly to release the dough onto the baking sheet. (If necessary, use a knife to pry the dough out of the mold.) Or, pat the dough into an 8-in/20-cm circle on a lightly greased baking sheet. With a fork, prick dough deeply to make 8 or 16 wedges.

Bake in a preheated 325°F/165°C/Gas Mark 3 oven for about 25 minutes, or till center of shortbread is set. While still warm, cut molded shortbread into wedges or cut hand-shaped shortbread along the perforations; remove shortbread from baking sheet and cool completely on a rack. If desired, sprinkle wedges with confectioners sugar.

Per wedge 188 calories/790 kilojoules, 2 g protein, 19 g carbohydrate, 12 g total fat (7 g saturated), 31 mg cholesterol, 170 mg sodium, 21 mg potassium

STEPS FOR SHAPING SHORTBREAD

STEP 1

Pressing into Mold

Press the dough into a prepared mold, working from the center to the edges. Be sure the dough fills every part of the mold. Gently pry the dough out of the mold, invert onto a greased baking sheet, and bake according to the recipe directions.

STEP 2

Shaping by Hand

Or, pat the dough into a circle on a greased baking sheet. Prick the dough deeply with a fork to divide it into 8 or 16 wedges. Use a ruler to make straight lines.

Raspberry-Orange Strips

These shortbread-like cookies are just as delicious filled with another flavor of jam.
We suggest using only butter for these delectable treats.
Its flavor is unmatched by any substitute.

INGREDIENTS

1¼ cups/5 oz/155 g all-purpose (plain) flour

3 tablespoons granulated sugar

1 teaspoon finely shredded orange peel

½ cup/4 oz/125 g cold butter

¼ cup/2½ oz/75 g seedless raspberry jam

½ cup/2 oz/60 g flaked almonds, chopped pistachios, or pine nuts

Preparation Time 20 minutes
Baking Time 20 to 25 minutes
Makes about 18 cookies

STEPS AT A GLANCE   Page

■ Cutting in butter
   or margarine   84

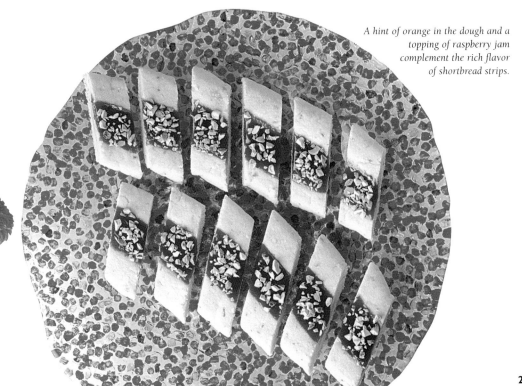

A hint of orange in the dough and a topping of raspberry jam complement the rich flavor of shortbread strips.

METHOD FOR MAKING RASPBERRY-ORANGE STRIPS

In a medium mixing bowl stir together the flour, sugar, and orange peel. Cut in the butter till mixture resembles fine crumbs. Form mixture into a ball and knead till smooth. Divide dough in half.

Shape each portion into an 8-in/20-cm roll. Place the rolls 4 to 5 in/10 to 12.5 cm apart on an ungreased baking sheet. Pat each roll into a 2-in/5-cm-wide strip. Using the back of a spoon, press a 1-in/2.5-cm-wide indentation lengthwise down the center of each strip. Bake in a preheated 325°F/ 165°C/Gas Mark 3 oven for 20 to 25 minutes, or till edges are lightly browned. Transfer the baking sheet to a cooling rack. Immediately spoon the jam into the indentations. While warm, cut rectangles diagonally into 1-in/2.5-cm-wide pieces. Sprinkle with nuts. Cool cookies completely on baking sheet.

Per cookie 115 calories/483 kilojoules, 2 g protein, 12 g carbohydrate, 7 g total fat (3 g saturated), 14 mg cholesterol, 53 mg sodium, 41 mg potassium

STEP 1

Making Indentations

Pat each roll of dough into a strip 2 in/5 cm wide. Press down the center of each strip with the back of a small spoon to create a 1-in/2.5-cm-wide indentation.

STEP 2

Cutting Strips

Bake the strips, transfer to a wire rack, then immediately fill the indentations with jam. While the strips are still warm, cut them diagonally with a sharp knife into 1-in/2.5-cm-wide pieces. Sprinkle with nuts and cool completely.

Shaped and Molded Cookies

229

Thin drizzles of white and dark chocolate are easily applied to these coated cookies by letting the melted topping fall from the tip of a spoon in a zigzag pattern.

Chocolate-Kahlúa Truffle Cookies

These no-bake cookies are quick, easy, and impressive, and almost any
of your favorite liqueurs can be used to make them. Try hazelnut,
orange, Irish cream, or chocolate flavors.

INGREDIENTS

2¹/₂ cups/7¹/₂ oz/235 g finely crushed
chocolate wafers or plain cookie crumbs

1 cup/4 oz/125 g finely chopped walnuts,
pecans, pine nuts, almonds, or hazelnuts

1 cup/4 oz/125 g sifted confectioners
(icing) sugar

¹/₃ cup/3 fl oz/80 ml Kahlúa or
other liqueur

1 to 2 tablespoons water

²/₃ cup/5 oz/155 g semisweet (plain)
chocolate, chopped

1 tablespoon solid vegetable shortening

1 cup/6 oz/185 g white chocolate,
chopped

METHOD FOR MAKING CHOCOLATE-KAHLÚA TRUFFLE COOKIES

Preparation Time 1 hour
Chilling Time 30 minutes
Makes about 30 cookies

In a large mixing bowl stir together the chocolate wafer crumbs, chopped nuts, confectioners sugar, and Kahlúa or other liqueur. Add enough of the water so crumbs hold together. Shape mixture into 1-in/2.5-cm balls. Place on a waxed paper-lined baking sheet.

In a small, heavy saucepan heat semisweet (plain) chocolate and shortening over low heat till melted. In another small, heavy saucepan heat white chocolate till melted. With a fork, dip half the cookies into the dark chocolate mixture to coat; place on baking sheet. Dip remaining cookies in melted white chocolate to coat; place on baking sheet.

With the tip of a spoon, thinly drizzle white chocolate mixture in a zigzag pattern over cookies coated with dark chocolate. Repeat with dark chocolate, drizzling over cookies coated with white chocolate mixture. Refrigerate for about 30 minutes, or till chocolate is firm. Store in refrigerator.

Per cookie: 147 calories/617 kilojoules, 2 g protein, 18 g carbohydrate, 7 g total fat (2 g saturated), 1 mg cholesterol, 72 mg sodium, 58 mg potassium

About Pine Nuts

Not actually a nut at all, the pine nut is the edible seed from the cones of several varieties of pine trees that are native to the United States, Mexico and southern Europe. In Spain, Turkey, Greece, Italy and Lebanon, pine nuts are used extensively in sweet dishes, and in savory dishes too, the most famous of which is the Genoese sauce, *pesto*. They can be found in most supermarkets, packaged, and ready to eat.

Pine nuts are softer and oilier than most other nuts and are at their best when lightly toasted. This can be done in the oven or in a dry frying pan. But beware—pine nuts turn from golden to burnt in an instant. Watch them carefully while they toast and shake the pan often so they brown evenly. Because of their high oil content, pine nuts become rancid even more quickly than other nuts. Buy small quantities and store them in an airtight container in the refrigerator. Or, if buying in bulk, store them in the freezer until needed.

Pine nuts can be used interchangeably with other nuts, but their taste is more subtle, and because their extraction from the pine cones is so labor-intensive, they are more expensive.

Pecan Florentines

These lacy cookies are buttery and crisp. Don't bake more than 5 cookies on the baking
sheet at one time because even a tiny amount of cookie batter will spread a lot.

INGREDIENTS

1/4 cup/2 oz/60 g granulated
sugar

1/4 cup/2 oz/60 g butter or
margarine, melted

1 tablespoon molasses or
golden syrup

1 tablespoon milk

1/4 cup/1 oz/30 g ground pecans
or walnuts

1/4 cup/1 oz/30 g all-purpose
(plain) flour

1/3 cup/2 oz/60 g sweet cooking
chocolate or white chocolate

Preparation Time 20 minutes
Baking Time 5 to 6 minutes
Makes about 36 cookies

STEPS AT A GLANCE   Page

Drizzling icing or chocolate **22**

■ Grinding nuts   **45**

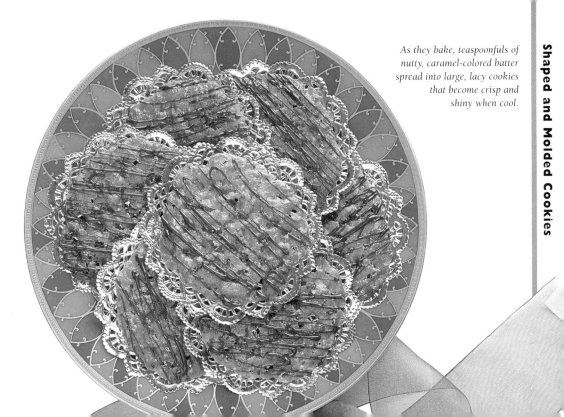

As they bake, teaspoonfuls of nutty, caramel-colored batter spread into large, lacy cookies that become crisp and shiny when cool.

METHOD FOR MAKING PECAN FLORENTINES

Line baking sheets with foil. Grease the foil. Set baking sheets aside.

In a medium mixing bowl stir together the sugar, melted butter or margarine, molasses or golden syrup, and milk. Stir in the ground pecans or walnuts and flour.

Drop level teaspoons of batter 5 in/13 cm apart onto a prepared baking sheet. (Bake only 3 to 5 cookies at a time.) Bake in a preheated 350°F/180°C/Gas Mark 4 oven for 5 to 6 minutes, or till bubbly and deep golden brown. Cool cookies on baking sheet for 1 to 2 minutes, or till set. Quickly remove from pan and cool on a rack. Repeat to bake remaining cookies.

In a small, heavy saucepan melt chocolate or white chocolate over low heat. Drizzle over cookies.

Per cookie 90 calories/378 kilojoules, 1 g protein, 10 g carbohydrate, 5 g total fat (1 g saturated), 3 mg cholesterol, 68 mg sodium, 22 mg potassium

Peanut Butter Bonbons

We call these bonbons because they have the look and richness
of melt-in-your-mouth candies, but they are easy to make.

INGREDIENTS

1/2 cup/4 oz/125 g butter or
margarine, softened

1/2 cup/4 oz/125 g crunchy
peanut butter

3/4 cup/6 oz/185 g packed
brown sugar

1/4 teaspoon baking soda

1 egg

1 1/2 teaspoons vanilla extract

2 1/2 cups/10 oz/315 g all-purpose
(plain) flour

2 cups/12 oz/375 g semisweet
(plain) chocolate, chopped

2 teaspoons solid
vegetable shortening

Luscious peanut butter cookie balls get a smooth coat from a dip in melted chocolate.

METHOD FOR MAKING PEANUT BUTTER BONBONS

Preparation Time 30 minutes
Baking Time 8 to 10 minutes
Makes about 52 bonbons

In a large mixing bowl beat the butter or margarine and peanut butter with an electric mixer on medium to high speed for 30 seconds. Add the brown sugar and baking soda; beat till combined. Beat in the egg and vanilla. Beat in as much of the flour as you can with the mixer. Stir in any remaining flour with a wooden spoon.

Shape dough into 1-in/2.5-cm balls. Place balls 1½ in/4 cm apart on ungreased baking sheets.

Bake in a preheated 350°F/180°C/Gas Mark 4 oven for 8 to 10 minutes, or till cookies are set and lightly browned on the bottom. Remove cookies from pan and cool on a rack.

In a medium, heavy saucepan heat chocolate and shortening over low heat till melted. Cool slightly. Using a fork, dip peanut butter balls, one at a time, into chocolate mixture to coat. Transfer to waxed paper–lined baking sheets. Chill till firm. Store airtight in a cool place.

Per bonbon 96 calories/403 kilojoules, 2 g protein, 12 g carbohydrate, 5 g total fat (1 g saturated), 9 mg cholesterol, 41 mg sodium, 58 mg potassium

Shaped and Molded Cookies

239

Cinnamon Snails

Children will love to decorate these cinnamon-scented snails almost as much as they will love to eat them.

INGREDIENTS

³/₄ cup/6 oz/185 g butter or margarine, softened

³/₄ cup/6 oz/185 g packed brown sugar

1 teaspoon ground cinnamon

¹/₄ teaspoon baking powder

1 egg

1 teaspoon vanilla extract

2 cups/8 oz/250 g all-purpose (plain) flour

1 tablespoon granulated sugar

¹/₂ teaspoon ground cinnamon

1 lightly beaten egg white

96 miniature semisweet (plain) chocolate chips (optional)

Preparation Time 20 minutes
Baking Time 8 minutes
Makes about 48 cookies

STEPS AT A GLANCE	Page
Making cookie dough	12–17
Making ropes	213

240

Brown-sugar cookie "snails", shaped by hand and decorated with chocolate-chip "eyes", make delightful treats for children.

METHOD FOR MAKING CINNAMON SNAILS

In a mixing bowl beat the butter or margarine with an electric mixer on medium to high speed for 30 seconds. Add the brown sugar, 1 teaspoon cinnamon, and baking powder; beat till combined. Beat in the egg and vanilla. Beat in as much of the flour as you can with the mixer. Stir in any remaining flour with a wooden spoon. Divide dough in half.

In a small mixing bowl stir together the granulated sugar and 1/2 teaspoon cinnamon. Set aside.

On a lightly floured surface, shape each half of the dough into a 12-in/30-cm log. Cut each log into twenty-four 1/2-in/12-mm pieces. Roll each piece into a 6-in/15-cm rope. Coil each rope into a snail shape, using one end to make a small coil for the eye, and coiling the other end in the opposite direction to make the body. Place the cookies 2 in/5 cm apart on lightly greased baking sheets. Brush each with egg white. Sprinkle with sugar-cinnamon mixture. If desired, insert 2 chocolate chips in the small coiled end for the eyes.

Bake in a preheated 375°F/190°C/Gas Mark 4 oven for 8 minutes, or till edges of the cookies are firm and the bottoms are lightly browned. Remove cookies from pan and cool on a rack.

Per cookie 59 calories/248 kilojoules, 1 g protein, 7 g carbohydrate, 3 g total fat (2 g saturated), 12 mg cholesterol, 36 mg sodium, 20 mg potassium

Lemon-Pistachio Pretzels

If you want to make these sweet pretzels even more delicate, grind the nuts
in a blender or food processor instead of just chopping them.

INGREDIENTS

¾ cup/6 oz/185 g butter or
margarine, softened

1 cup/4 oz/125 g sifted
confectioners (icing) sugar

2 teaspoons finely shredded
lemon peel

1 egg

½ teaspoon lemon extract

2 cups/8 oz/250 g all-purpose
(plain) flour

1½ cups/6 oz/185 g sifted
confectioners (icing) sugar

1 tablespoon lemon juice

1 to 2 tablespoons water

⅓ cup/2 oz/60 g finely
chopped pistachios,
walnuts, or almonds

Preparation Time 25 minutes
Chilling Time 30 to 60 minutes
Baking Time 8 to 10 minutes
Makes about 48 cookies

Sweet, buttery cookie pretzels are smoothly glazed with a lemon icing, then sprinkled with chopped pistachios for textural contrast.

METHOD FOR MAKING LEMON-PISTACHIO PRETZELS

In a mixing bowl beat butter or margarine with an electric mixer on medium to high speed for 30 seconds. Add 1 cup/4 oz/125 g confectioners sugar and lemon peel; beat till combined. Beat in egg and lemon extract. Beat in as much of the flour as you can with the mixer. Stir in any remaining flour with a wooden spoon. Divide dough in half. If necessary, cover and chill for 30 to 60 minutes, or till dough is easy to handle.

On a lightly floured surface, shape each half of the dough into a 12-in/30-cm log. Cut each log into twenty-four 1/2-in/12-mm pieces. Roll each piece into an 8-in/20-cm rope. Form each rope into a pretzel shape by crossing one end over the other to form a circle, overlapping them about 1 in/2.5 cm from each end. Bring the ends down to the opposite edge of the circle and press lightly to seal. Place pretzels about 2 in/5 cm apart on lightly greased baking sheets.

Bake in a preheated 375°F/190°C/Gas Mark 4 oven for 8 to 10 minutes, or till golden brown. Remove from pan and cool on a rack.

In a small bowl stir together 1 1/2 cups/6 oz/185 g confectioners sugar, lemon juice and enough water to make a mixture of glazing consistency. Brush cookies with glaze; sprinkle with pistachios or other nuts. Let stand till set.

Per pretzel 78 calories/328 kilojoules, 1 g protein, 11 g carbohydrate, 3 g total fat (2 g saturated), 12 mg cholesterol, 35 mg sodium, 17 mg potassium

Koulourakia

When visiting a Greek home, you might be welcomed with this licorice-flavored cookie along with a small cup of strong coffee and a glass of cold water.

INGREDIENTS

3/4 cup/6 oz/185 g butter or margarine, softened

3/4 cup/6 oz/185 g granulated sugar

2 teaspoons baking powder

1 teaspoon aniseed

1 teaspoon finely shredded lemon peel

2 eggs

2 tablespoons milk

3 cups/12 oz/375 g all-purpose (plain) flour

1 lightly beaten egg white

1 tablespoon milk

3 tablespoons sesame seeds (optional)

Preparation Time 30 minutes
Chilling Time 30 to 60 minutes
Baking Time 7 to 9 minutes
Makes about 48 cookies

STEPS AT A GLANCE	Page
Making cookie dough	12–17
Making ropes	213

Letter-shaped cookies like these aniseeed-flavored ones from Greece are also traditional in Scandinavia.

METHOD FOR MAKING KOULOURAKIA

In a large mixing bowl beat the butter or margarine with an electric mixer on medium to high speed for 30 seconds. Add the sugar, baking powder, aniseed, and lemon peel; beat till combined. Beat in the eggs and 2 tablespoons milk. Beat in as much of the flour as you can with the mixer. Stir in any remaining flour with a wooden spoon. Divide dough in half. If necessary, chill dough for 30 to 60 minutes, or till firm and easy to handle.

On a lightly floured surface, shape each half of dough into a 12-in/30-cm log. Cut each log into twenty-four 1/2-in/12-mm pieces. Roll each piece into a 6-in/15-cm rope. Curl each end of the rope to form an S shape. Place the cookies 1 in/2.5 cm apart on greased baking sheets.

In a small mixing bowl stir together egg white and 1 tablespoon milk; brush mixture over cookies. If desired, sprinkle cookies with sesame seed.

Bake in a preheated 375°F/190°C/Gas Mark 4 oven for 7 to 9 minutes, or till bottoms are lightly browned. Remove cookies from pans and cool on a rack.

Per cookie 67 calories/281 kilojoules, 1 g protein, 9 g carbohydrate, 3 g total fat (1 g saturated), 19 mg cholesterol, 39 mg sodium, 15 mg potassium

Sesame Fork Cookies

These may look like old-fashioned peanut butter cookies, but their texture and flavor is deliciously updated with tahini (sesame paste).

INGREDIENTS

³/₄ cup/6 oz/185 g butter or margarine, softened

1 cup/7 oz/220 g packed brown sugar

1¹/₂ teaspoons baking powder

¹/₄ teaspoon ground nutmeg

1 egg

3 tablespoons tahini (sesame paste) or peanut butter

1 teaspoon vanilla extract

1 cup/4 oz/125 g wholemeal flour

1²/₃ cups/7 oz/220 g all-purpose (plain) flour

¹/₃ cup/1 oz/30 g sesame seeds

Preparation Time 35 minutes
Baking Time 7 to 9 minutes
Makes about 70 cookies

Tahini instead of the usual peanut butter adds an exotic, unexpected flavor to these easily prepared cookies.

METHOD FOR MAKING SESAME FORK COOKIES

In a large mixing bowl beat the butter or margarine with an electric mixer on medium to high speed for 30 seconds. Add the brown sugar, baking powder, and nutmeg; beat till combined. Beat in the egg, tahini or peanut butter, and vanilla. Beat in the wholemeal flour and as much of the all-purpose flour as you can with the mixer. Stir in any remaining all-purpose flour and the sesame seed with a wooden spoon. Shape dough into 1-in/2.5-cm balls. Place 2 in/5 cm apart on ungreased baking sheets. Flatten each ball by pressing with the tines of a fork in a crisscross pattern.

Bake in a preheated 375°F/190°C/Gas Mark 4 oven for 7 to 9 minutes, or till lightly browned. Remove cookies from the pans and cool on a rack.

Per cookie 52 calories/218 kilojoules, 1 g protein, 7 g carbohydrate, 3 g total fat (1 g saturated), 8 mg cholesterol, 26 mg sodium, 27 mg potassium

Shaped and Molded Cookies

PRESSED COOKIES

Making Pressed Cookies

Pressed, or "spritz", cookies are an old Scandinavian speciality, but they have become a favorite in many other countries, too. Most cookie presses are simple devices that operate with either a lever-and-ratchet system or with a rotating screw top (an electric press is also available, but is a little more difficult to find). A removable coupler at the bottom of the container holds your choice of interchangeable design plates and, in some cases, plain or star-shaped nozzles. To use, secure the plate or nozzle, pack the dough into the container, and force it through the press onto a baking sheet. Out come little wreaths, miniature trees, dainty butterflies, delicate flowers, ridged ribbons, or any one of the dozens of patterns created by the manufacturer. The press does all the work and does it perfectly. All you do is make the dough, choose the design, and bake the result. As the shapes themselves are so decorative, the only finishing touch might be a sprinkling of glittering sugar crystals, a scattering of finely chopped nuts, colored sprinkles, or a chocolate tint in the dough. Always use room-temperature dough, as chilled dough is too stiff to push through the press easily.

For pressed cookies, you need the standard equipment for making and baking dough, plus an easy-to-operate cookie press that comes with an assortment of removable design plates.

mixing bowl

baking sheet and
small, sharp knife

rubber spatula

cookie press and plates

drop the plate in so that it rests flat in the holder

STEP 1

Putting Plate in Holder
Unscrew the holder from the bottom of the cookie press. Place a plate in the holder with the correct side facing up (as specified by the manufacturer's directions).

some recipes require a plain or star-shaped nozzle, which is also dropped into the holder

for a narrow press, use a narrow spatula to transfer the dough

STEP 2

Packing Press with Dough
Scoop up cookie dough with a rubber spatula and pack it into the container of the press. Don't leave any large air holes in the dough or the shapes will distort when pressed out. Screw on the holder and plate or nozzle.

don't let the
dough squeeze
out under the
press

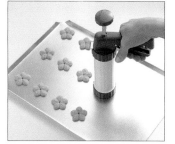

STEP 3

Forcing Dough through Press

For all shapes except ribbons (see step 4), hold the press straight down on an ungreased baking sheet. Force the dough through (it will stick to the baking sheet) and release the pressure just before you lift the press off the cookie.

lift up the press
when the cookie
is the desired
length

STEP 4

Making Ribbons

Hold the press at an angle. Draw the press along the ungreased baking sheet in a straight line as you force out the dough.

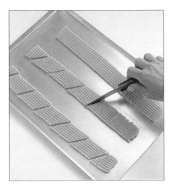

you can also cut strips with a rolling pastry wheel for straight or fluted edges

STEP 5

Making Diagonal Ribbons
Press out long strips of dough onto the baking sheet. Use a sharp knife to cut the strips at an angle, being careful not to cut too deeply so you will not mark the sheet.

With a simple cookie press and decorative plates or nozzles, you can create many shapes from the same dough. These cookies are made from the dough for Anise Butterflies on page 272.

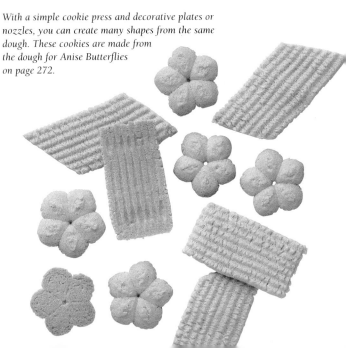

About Sprinkles and Crushed Nuts

There are unlimited toppings you can use to decorate cookies: colored candy sprinkles (nonpareils)—either in the shape of little logs or little balls, candied fruit, candy violets and rose petals, silver or other colored balls (dragees), tiny marshmallows, sugar-coated cumin seeds, candied orange and lemon slices, grated chocolate, chocolate flakes, chocolate chips, candies of all kinds, and of course, chopped and crushed nuts. Some toppings indicate the cookie's flavor: toasted shreds of coconut to show you it's a coconut cookie, sugar and spice mixed together to signal a spiced cookie, for example. All of them give cookies a festive look, especially important at children's parties and on holiday cookies.

Iced cookies should be sprinkled with their topping while still slightly sticky so that the topping will adhere. If you put the topping on before the cookie is baked, press it firmly into the dough. Use hearty toppings such as chopped nuts and chocolate chips on big lumpy cookies; keep tiny delicate sprinkles and candied flowers for dainty tea cookies.

*The ridged half-moons were shaped with a
cookie press fitted with a star nozzle,
while the smooth ones were made
with a plain nozzle.*

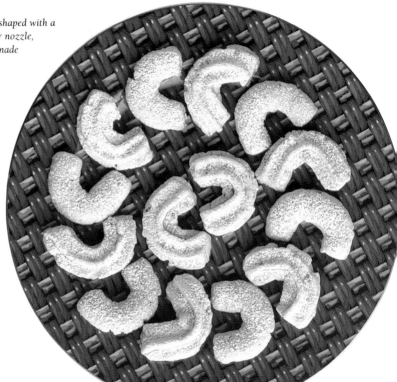

Almond Half-Moons

These crisp little cookies, reminiscent of Chinese almond cookies, will taste good in any shape your cookie press makes, but be sure to choose a nozzle with at least a ½-in/12-mm opening—the ground nuts might get caught in a smaller opening.

INGREDIENTS

1 cup/8 oz/250 g butter or margarine, softened

½ cup/4 oz/125 g granulated sugar

1 egg

¼ teaspoon almond extract

2¼ cups/9 oz/280 g all-purpose (plain) flour

¾ cup/3 oz/90 g ground almonds, hazelnuts, or pecans

sifted confectioners (icing) sugar

Preparation Time 30 minutes
Baking Time 6 to 8 minutes
Makes about 70 biscuits

METHOD FOR MAKING ALMOND HALF-MOONS

In a large mixing bowl beat the butter or margarine with an electric mixer on medium to high speed for 30 seconds. Add the sugar; beat till combined. Beat in the egg and almond extract. Beat in as much of the flour as you can with the mixer. Stir in any remaining flour and the ground nuts with a wooden spoon. Do not chill dough.

Pack dough into a cookie press fitted with a ½-in/12-mm-wide round or star nozzle. Force dough through the press 1 in/2.5 cm apart onto ungreased baking sheets forming crescent shapes.

Bake in a preheated 375°F/190°C/Gas Mark 4 oven for 6 to 8 minutes, or till edges are firm and bottoms are lightly browned. Remove cookies from pans and cool on a rack. Sprinkle cookies with confectioners sugar.

Per cookie 52 calories/218 kilojoules, 1 g protein, 5 g carbohydrate, 3 g total fat (2 g saturated), 10 mg cholesterol, 32 mg sodium, 16 mg potassium

STEP 1

Bending Dough

Press out 3 long strips of dough on an ungreased baking sheet through a ½-in/12-mm nozzle. Cut each strip into 2½-in/6-cm lengths. To make a half-moon, press a finger in the middle of one length of dough while pushing the ends in the other direction.

Chocolate Butter Spritz

If you're in a hurry, you can also make these as drop cookies simply by dropping
rounded teaspoonfuls of the dough onto the baking sheets.

INGREDIENTS

1 cup/8 oz/250 g butter or margarine, softened

1/2 cup/2 oz/60 g sifted confectioners (icing) sugar

1/2 cup/3 1/2 oz/105 g packed brown sugar

1/4 cup/3/4 oz/20 g unsweetened cocoa powder

1 egg yolk

2 tablespoons crème de cacao or milk

1 teaspoon vanilla extract

2 1/3 cups/10 oz/315 g all-purpose (plain) flour

chocolate sprinkles or finely chopped nuts (optional)

Preparation Time 25 minutes
Baking Time 8 to 10 minutes
Makes about 60 cookies

STEPS AT A GLANCE	Page
Making cookie dough	12–17
Making pressed cookies	254–258

The bumpy cracks and crevices of festive spritz cookies trap chunks of nuts and bits of decorative chocolate sprinkles.

METHOD FOR MAKING CHOCOLATE BUTTER SPRITZ

In a large mixing bowl beat the butter or margarine with an electric mixer on medium to high speed for 30 seconds. Add the confectioners sugar, brown sugar, and cocoa powder; beat till combined. Beat in the egg yolk, crème de cacao or milk, and vanilla. Beat in as much of the flour as you can with the mixer. Stir in any remaining flour with a wooden spoon. Do not chill dough.

Pack the dough into a cookie press fitted with desired plate. Force dough through press 1 in/2.5 cm apart onto ungreased baking sheets. If desired, sprinkle with chocolate sprinkles or chopped nuts.

Bake in a preheated 375°F/190°C/Gas Mark 4 oven for 8 to 10 minutes, or till edges of cookies are firm but not brown. Remove cookies from pans and cool on a rack.

Per cookie 58 calories/244 kilojoules, 1 g protein, 7 g carbohydrate, 3 g total fat (2 g saturated), 9 mg cholesterol, 37 mg sodium, 13 mg potassium

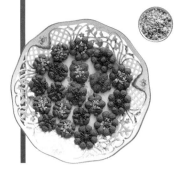

STEP I

Sprinkling

Prepare the chocolate dough and pack it into a cookie press. Press out cookies onto ungreased baking sheets using one or more decorative plates. Sprinkle the unbaked cookies with chocolate sprinkles or finely chopped nuts. As the cookies bake, the toppings will stick to them.

These old-fashioned ridged cookies were easily formed with a cookie press fitted with a ribbon plate, then decorated with glistening sugar crystals and almonds.

Glazed Almond Strips

As an alternative to making several 2½-in/6-cm strips with the cookie press,
you can make one long strip and then cut it into the correct lengths with a knife.

INGREDIENTS

¾ cup/6 oz/185 g butter or
margarine, softened

½ cup/3½ oz/105 g packed
brown sugar

2 teaspoons milk

few drops almond extract

1¾ cups/7 oz/220 g all-purpose
(plain) flour

1 lightly beaten egg white

½ cup/2 oz/60 g flaked almonds
or pine nuts

1 teaspoon granulated sugar

Preparation Time 30 minutes
Baking Time 7 to 8 minutes
Makes about 54 cookies

STEPS AT A GLANCE	Page
Making cookie dough	**12–17**
Making pressed cookies	**254–258**

METHOD FOR MAKING GLAZED ALMOND STRIPS

In a mixing bowl beat the butter or margarine with an electric mixer on medium to high speed for 30 seconds. Add the brown sugar, milk, and almond extract; beat till combined. Mix in as much of the flour as you can with the mixer. Stir in any remaining flour with a wooden spoon. Do not chill dough.

Pack the dough into a cookie press fitted with a ribbon plate. Force dough through cookie press onto ungreased baking sheets, making 2¹/₂-in/6-cm ribbons about 1 in/2.5 cm apart. Using a pastry brush, brush each cookie with egg white, then sprinkle with almonds or pine nuts and granulated sugar.

Bake in a preheated 375°F/190°C/Gas Mark 4 oven for 7 to 8 minutes, or till edges are firm but not brown. Let cool 1 minute on baking sheets. Remove cookies and cool on a rack.

Per cookie 50 calories/210 kilojoules, 1 g protein, 5 g carbohydrate, 3 g total fat (2 g saturated), 7 mg cholesterol, 32 mg sodium, 21 mg potassium

STEP 1

Brushing Glaze

Lightly beat the egg white and brush it on each cookie with a pastry brush, making sure that it fills the ridges. The glaze will give the cookies a subtle sheen and will serve as "glue" for the nut topping.

STEP 2

Adding Almonds

After the cookies have been brushed with egg white, arrange almonds decoratively on each. If desired, the design can differ from cookie to cookie. Sprinkle with sugar, and bake.

Anise Butterflies

Making spritz cookies will go more smoothly if you pack the dough firmly into the cookie press. This eliminates any air pockets that could leave holes in the shapes.

INGREDIENTS

3/4 cup/6 oz/185 g butter or margarine, softened

1/2 cup/3 1/2 oz/105 g packed brown sugar

1/2 teaspoon baking powder

1/4 teaspoon ground cinnamon

1/8 teaspoon ground ginger

1 egg yolk

1 teaspoon anise extract

1 3/4 cups/7 oz/220 g all-purpose (plain) flour

Preparation Time 15 minutes
Baking Time 8 to 10 minutes
Makes about 60 cookies

STEPS AT A GLANCE   Page

▢ Making cookie dough   **12–17**
■ Making pressed
   cookies   254–258

Butterflies and other elaborate designs are easy to make with a cookie press.

METHOD FOR MAKING ANISE BUTTERFLIES

In a large mixing bowl beat the butter or margarine with an electric mixer on medium to high speed for 30 seconds. Add the brown sugar, baking powder, cinnamon, and ginger; beat till combined. Beat in the egg yolk and anise extract. Beat in as much of the flour as you can with the mixer. Stir in any remaining flour with a wooden spoon. Do not chill dough.

Pack the dough into a cookie press fitted with a butterfly plate. Force dough through press 1 in/2.5 cm apart onto ungreased baking sheets.

Bake in a preheated 375°F/190°C/Gas Mark 4 oven for 8 to 10 minutes, or till edges of cookies are firm but not brown. Remove cookies from pans and cool on a rack.

Per cookie 41 calories/172 kilojoules, 0 g protein, 4 g carbohydrate, 2 g total fat (1 g saturated), 10 mg cholesterol, 28 mg sodium, 12 mg potassium

Lemon-Ginger Tea Cookies

Don't use cookie-press plates with very small openings for this recipe;
the grated lemon peel may clog up the openings.

INGREDIENTS

1 1/2 cups/12 oz/375 g butter or
margarine, softened

1 cup/8 oz/250 g granulated
sugar

1 tablespoon grated lemon peel

1 teaspoon ground ginger

1/8 teaspoon ground cloves

1 egg

1 teaspoon lemon juice

3 1/2 cups/14 oz/440 g
all-purpose (plain) flour

slivered candied
(crystallized) ginger
(optional)

candied lemon peel (optional)

Preparation Time 20 minutes
Baking Time 8 to 10 minutes
Makes about 100 cookies

METHOD FOR MAKING LEMON-GINGER TEA COOKIES

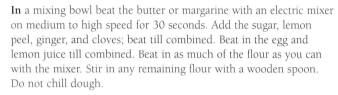

Bits of candied ginger and candied lemon peel top these cookies and give a hint of their flavor.

In a mixing bowl beat the butter or margarine with an electric mixer on medium to high speed for 30 seconds. Add the sugar, lemon peel, ginger, and cloves; beat till combined. Beat in the egg and lemon juice till combined. Beat in as much of the flour as you can with the mixer. Stir in any remaining flour with a wooden spoon. Do not chill dough.

Pack dough into a cookie press fitted with the desired plate (we've used three different plates). Force dough 1 in/2.5 cm apart onto ungreased baking sheets. If desired, decorate cookies with slivered candied ginger and/or candied lemon peel.

Bake in a preheated 375°F/190°C/Gas Mark 4 oven for 8 to 10 minutes, or till edges are set and beginning to brown. Remove cookies from pans and cool on a rack.

Per cookie 47 calories/197 kilojoules, 1 g protein, 5 g carbohydrate, 3 g total fat (2 g saturated), 9 mg cholesterol, 33 mg sodium, 7 mg potassium

Orange Marmalade Wreaths

Dress up these wreaths by drizzling melted chocolate over them. For the Christmas season, press snipped pieces of red and green maraschino cherries into the drizzled chocolate while it's still warm.

INGREDIENTS

COOKIES

1 cup/8 oz/250 g butter or margarine, softened

3/4 cup/3 oz/90 g sifted confectioners (icing) sugar

2 teaspoons grated orange peel

2 cups/8 oz/250 g all-purpose (plain) flour

FILLING

1/3 cup/3 oz/90 g cream cheese, softened

2 tablespoons orange marmalade

DRIZZLE (OPTIONAL)

1/4 cup/1 1/2 oz/450 g semisweet (plain) chocolate, chopped

1/2 teaspoon solid vegetable shortening

Festive cookie wreaths, filled with rich cream cheese and orange marmalade and drizzled with chocolate, will brighten any cookie assortment.

METHOD FOR MAKING ORANGE MARMALADE WREATHS

Preparation Time: 30 minutes
Baking Time 7 to 9 minutes
Makes about 20 cookies

For cookies, in a large mixing bowl beat the butter or margarine with an electric mixer on medium to high speed for 30 seconds. Add the confectioners sugar and orange peel; beat till combined. Beat in as much of the flour as you can with the mixer. Stir in any remaining flour with a wooden spoon. Do not chill the dough.

Pack dough into a cookie press fitted with a wreath plate. Force dough through the cookie press in wreath shapes 1 in/2.5 cm apart onto ungreased baking sheets.

Bake in a preheated 375°F/190°C/Gas Mark 4 oven for 7 to 9 minutes, or till edges are firm but not brown. Remove cookies from pans and cool on a rack.

For filling, in a small mixing bowl stir together the cream cheese and orange marmalade. Spread 1 teaspoon of the cream cheese-marmalade mixture over the flat side of half the cookies; top with remaining cookies, flat sides down.

If desired, for drizzle, in a small, heavy saucepan melt chocolate and shortening over low heat. Drizzle over cookies.

Per cookie 159 calories/668 kilojoules, 2 g protein, 14 g carbohydrate, 11 g total fat (7 g saturated), 25 mg cholesterol, 121 mg sodium, 23 mg potassium

About Candied Peel

The best candied peel is made in large strips. It is boiled in sugar syrup, left to cool, and boiled again with more sugar added to the syrup. This process is repeated several times with more sugar added each time until a 70 percent syrup is obtained. The peel is left in the syrup for a week, then it is air-dried, coated in granulated sugar and cut into thin slices. No essential oils are lost and the peel remains soft and juicy. And prepared in this way, the fruit needs no preservatives or other chemical additives—the sugar preserves it. Orange, lemon, lime and citron can all be candied. The chopped candied peel we buy at the supermarket hasn't been made in this traditional way, but if you like candied peel in your cookies, it's worth looking for the real thing in health food stores and gourmet food shops.

Even though candied peel is coated in sugar, it adds a little tartness to cookies, and a little chewiness too. Chop it finely and sprinkle it on still-sticky lemon or orange icing. Store candied peel in the freezer for maximum freshness.

SPECIAL COOKIES

BASIC TOOLS FOR MAKING MADELEINES

You'll need bowls and a rubber spatula for
mixing the batter, a pastry brush and a
madeleine mold for baking, and a rack and
mesh sieve for finishing the cookies.

mixing bowls and
fine-meshed sieve

wire rack

madeleine
mold

rubber spatula

knife

pastry brush

Making Madeleines

Delicate madeleines, like the other cookies in this chapter, aren't easily categorized. These French tea cookies resemble tiny sponge cakes, yet they are not baked in a cake pan. Instead they are formed in small shell-shaped molds that each produces a single portion. But no matter what you call them, the result is an ethereal dessert, especially when eaten soon after they cool.

Traditional madeleine molds are made of tinned steel and are available in hardware or department stores or from shops that specialize in cooking equipment. A pan for standard-size madeleines like those shown on the following pages typically has 12 molds, each 3 in/7.5 cm long from the top of the shell to its base. Before baking, the molds must be brushed with melted butter or margarine so the fragile cookies can be released easily after baking.

Madeleines will be especially light, airy, and moist if you keep two simple hints in mind when you prepare them. First, beat the sugar and eggs thoroughly (at least 5 minutes or more) until the mixture makes a thick, satiny ribbon on the surface of the batter when the beaters are lifted. Second, blend the batter with care so it doesn't deflate, especially when folding in the dry ingredients.

Spiced Madeleines

Part sponge cake, part cookie, sugar-dusted madeleines are a classic French confection. Serve them in the afternoon with a cup of tea.

INGREDIENTS

4 eggs

1 teaspoon vanilla extract

2/3 cup/5 oz/155 g granulated sugar

1 1/3 cups/5 1/2 oz/170 g all-purpose (plain) flour

1 teaspoon ground cinnamon

1/2 teaspoon baking powder

1/4 teaspoon ground nutmeg

1/2 cup/4 oz/125 g margarine or butter, melted and cooled

confectioners (icing) sugar

Preparation Time 30 minutes
Baking Time 10 to 12 minutes
Makes about 30 madeleines

In a large mixing bowl beat eggs and vanilla with an electric mixer on high speed for 5 minutes. Gradually beat in the sugar. Beat for 5 to 7 minutes, or till thick and satiny.

In a medium mixing bowl sift together the flour, cinnamon, baking powder, and nutmeg. Sift one-quarter of the flour mixture over the egg mixture; gently fold in. Fold in the remaining flour by quarters. Fold in the butter or margarine. Spoon the batter into greased madeleine molds, filling each one three-quarters full.

Bake in a preheated 375°F/190°C/Gas Mark 4 oven for 10 to 12 minutes, or till edges are golden and tops spring back. Cool in molds on a rack for 1 minute.

Transfer madeleines to a rack and cool. Sift confectioners sugar over tops. Store in freezer.

Per madeleine 75 calories/315 kilojoules, 1 g protein, 9 g carbohydrate, 4 g total fat (2 g saturated), 37 mg cholesterol, 45 mg sodium, 16 mg potassium

STEPS FOR MAKING SPICED MADELEINES

the bristles of a pastry brush will reach every crevice of the mold

STEP 1

Greasing Molds

With a pastry brush, completely coat each madeleine mold with melted butter or margarine, making sure that each groove is coated so the finished cookies won't stick to the pan. Or spray with nonstick spray coating.

the two mixtures will blend more easily if only a portion of the dry ingredients is added at a time

STEP 2

Folding Flour into Eggs

Sift one-quarter of the flour mixture over the egg mixture. Gently fold by cutting down through the center with the edge of a rubber spatula, coming across the bottom of the bowl, then lifting up along the side of the bowl in one smooth motion.

you can also
invert the mold
over the wire
rack to remove
the cookies, but
they may be
damaged
as they fall out

STEP 3

Removing Madeleines
After the cookies have finished baking, let them cool in
the pan for 1 minute. Loosen each cookie with a knife or
skewer, then lift it out of the pan and place on a wire
rack to cool completely.

you can also use a
confectioners-
sugar canister to
apply the topping

STEP 4

Sifting Confectioners Sugar
Place all the madeleines ridged-side up on
the rack. Spoon some confectioners sugar into a fine-
meshed sieve or perforated canister and tap it
to lightly dust the tops of the cookies.

Part of the charm of madeleines is their scalloped shape, but if you don't have a madeleine mold, you can bake them in small tartlet pans.

About Proust and Madeleines

Madeleines, little shell-shaped cakes, cooked in special madeleine molds, were made famous by the French writer Marcel Proust in his seven-volume novel, *Remembrance of Things Past*.

The middle-aged narrator is drinking a cup of tea into which he has dipped a madeleine when suddenly he is flooded with memories of his boyhood holidays in the village of Combray. He remembers the landscape and the people, and this is the starting point of his long journey into the past.

Because of *Remembrance of Things Past*, madeleines have become one of the most famous foods in all literature.

Madeleines were invented in the little town of Commercy in the province of Lorraine in northern France and are thought to have been the work of a cook called Madeleine Paumier. They are a great favorite with French children.

Almond and Cherry Microwave Cookies

When you're in a hurry, microwave these peanut butter-flavored cookies and decorate with a glacé cherry or an almond.

INGREDIENTS

1/2 cup/4 oz/125 g peanut butter

1/4 cup/2 oz/60 g butter or margarine

5 1/2 oz/170 g granulated sugar

1 egg

1/2 teaspoon almond extract

1 1/2 cups/6 oz/185 g all-purpose (plain) flour

1/2 teaspoon baking powder

6 glacé cherries, halved

12 blanched almonds

Preparation time 20 minutes
Baking time 2 minutes
Makes about 24 cookies

STEPS AT A GLANCE   Page

Making cookie dough   **12–17**

Shaping balls   **212**

Place peanut butter and butter or margarine into a large microwave-safe mixing bowl. Soften on high power for 15 seconds. Add the sugar and beat with an electric mixer on medium to high speed till the mixture until light and fluffy. Stir in the egg and almond extract and beat till combined. Stir in as much of the flour and baking powder as you can with the mixer. Stir in any remaining flour with a wooden spoon.

Shape teaspoons of dough into balls and place 6 balls, widely spaced, on a large greased microwave-safe plate. Flatten each dough ball lightly with the heel of your hand and place half a glacé cherry on half of them, and a blanched almond on the other half.

Cook on high power for 1¹/₂ to 2 minutes, until cooked through and set. Let stand for 1 to 2 minutes to crisp a little before removing to a wire rack to cool completely. Repeat with the rest of the dough.

Per cookie 113 calories/
474 kilojoules, 3 g protein,
14 g carbohydrate,
5 g total fat (2 g saturated),
14 mg cholesterol,
44 mg sodium,
62 mg potassium

Ladyfingers

These dainty and versatile sponge cakes can be made
into sandwiches with jam, used to line a dessert mold,
or simply served with fresh fruit and a cup of tea.

INGREDIENTS

4 egg whites

1/2 cup/2 oz/60 g sifted
confectioners (icing) sugar

4 egg yolks

1 teaspoon vanilla extract

3/4 cup/2 1/2 oz/75 g all-
purpose (plain) flour

4 teaspoons confectioners
(icing) sugar

*A coating of confectioners sugar melts into the fragrant dough as these
ladyfingers bake, infusing them with a wonderful depth of flavor.
Dust with sugar again before serving.*

Preparation Time 45 minutes
Baking Time 8 to 10 minutes
Makes about 36 ladyfingers

In a large mixing bowl let the egg whites stand at room temperature for 30 minutes. Line a baking sheet with parchment paper or greaseproof paper. Set aside. In a large mixing bowl beat egg whites with an electric mixer on high speed till soft peaks form (tips curl). Gradually add 1 oz/30 g of the confectioners sugar, beating till stiff peaks form (tips stand up).

In a small mixing bowl beat the egg yolks on medium speed for 1 minute. Gradually add the remaining confectioners sugar, beating on high speed till thick and lemon-colored, 4 to 5 minutes. Stir in vanilla. By hand, fold egg yolk mixture into egg whites. Gradually fold in flour. Spoon batter into a piping bag fitted with a large round nozzle (about ¹/₂ in/12 mm in diameter). Pipe 3¹/₂ x ³/₄-in/ 9 x 2-cm strips of batter 1 in/2.5 cm apart on the prepared baking sheet. (Or, spoon batter into lightly greased ladyfinger molds till batter is even with top of pan.) Sift 4 teaspoons confectioners sugar over top.

Bake in a preheated 350°F/180°C/Gas Mark 4 oven for 8 to 10 minutes, or till lightly browned. Transfer cookies on paper or in ladyfinger molds to a rack; cool about 10 minutes. Remove ladyfingers from the paper or molds, then cool completely on the rack. Store in the freezer.

Per ladyfinger 24 calories/101 kilojoules, 1 g protein, 4 g carbohydrate, 1 g total fat (0 g saturated), 24 mg cholesterol, 7 mg sodium, 10 mg potassium

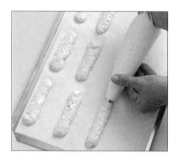

STEP 1

Piping Cookies

Line baking sheets with parchment paper or greaseproof paper. Spoon the batter into a piping bag fitted with a ½-in/12-mm round nozzle. Lay the bag almost parallel with the cookie sheet and, using even pressure, pipe out 3½x¾-in/9x2-cm strips of dough.

STEP 2

Sifting Sugar

Sprinkle the ladyfingers with confectioners sugar from a confectioners sugar canister or a fine-meshed sieve. Then bake.

Biscotti are baked twice to slowly dry them into the crunchy rusks that Italians enjoy dipped in coffee or Vin Santo, a sweet dessert wine.

Biscotti

Biscotti are a traditional Italian treat often served with strong, hot coffee.
The small, crisp slices are made for dunking. For a spiced version, omit
the almond extract and stir in ½ teaspoon ground cinnamon,
¼ teaspoon ground cloves, and ¼ teaspoon ground nutmeg.

INGREDIENTS

1 cup/8 oz/250 g granulated sugar

1 teaspoon baking soda

¼ teaspoon salt

3 eggs

1 teaspoon vanilla extract

½ teaspoon almond extract

2¾ cups/11 oz/345 g all-purpose (plain) flour

1 cup/5 oz/155 g finely chopped flaked almonds, walnuts, pecans, pine nuts, macadamia nuts, or hazelnuts

1 beaten egg

1 teaspoon water

METHOD FOR MAKING BISCOTTI

Preparation Time 35 minutes
Baking Time 40 to 43 minutes
Makes about 38 biscotti

In a large mixing bowl stir together the sugar, baking soda, and salt. Stir in 3 eggs, vanilla, and almond extract. Stir in the flour and chopped nuts.

On a well-floured surface, knead dough 8 to 10 times. Divide in half. On a lightly floured surface shape each half into a log about 9 in/23 cm long. Place logs about 4 in/10 cm apart on a lightly greased baking sheet. Pat each log into a flattened loaf about 10 in/25 cm long and 2¼ in/5.5 cm wide. Stir together the egg and water; brush over loaves.

Bake in a preheated 325°F/165°C/Gas Mark 3 oven for 30 minutes. Cool on a rack. Cut each loaf diagonally into ½-in/12-mm-thick slices. Place slices, cut-sides down, on ungreased baking sheets. Bake in the 325°F/165°C/Gas Mark 3 oven for 5 minutes. Turn slices over and bake for 5 to 8 minutes more, or till dry and crisp. Remove cookies from pan and cool on a rack.

Per biscotto 75 calories/315 kilojoules, 2 g protein, 12 g carbohydrate, 2 g total fat (0 g saturated), 22 mg cholesterol, 54 mg sodium, 37 mg potassium

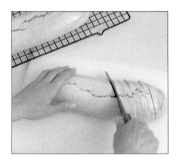

STEP 1

Cutting Loaves

Bake the loaves for 30 minutes, then cool. Place a loaf on a cutting board and slice diagonally into 1/2-in/12-mm-thick slices with a sharp, thin-bladed or serrated knife. Repeat with the other loaf.

STEP 2

Second Baking

Place the slices cut-side down on ungreased baking sheets. Bake for 5 minutes, then turn them over and bake until the biscotti are dry and crisp, another 5 to 8 minutes. Cool them on a wire rack.

Special Cookies

Chocolate-dipped Mushrooms

If you want spotted mushrooms, use a toothpick or a small, new paintbrush to "paint" spots of melted chocolate on the mushroom caps. Try to make these cookies on a cool, dry day, as humidity or rain tends to make meringue soft or cause it to bead.

INGREDIENTS

3 egg whites

1/2 teaspoon vanilla extract

1/4 teaspoon cream of tartar

3/4 cup/6 oz/185 g granulated sugar

2/3 cup/4 oz/125 g semisweet (plain) chocolate, chopped

2 tablespoons sifted confectioners (icing) sugar

2 teaspoons unsweetened cocoa powder

Preparation Time 45 minutes
Baking Time 20 to 25 minutes
Drying Time 30 minutes
Makes about 55 cookies

STEPS AT A GLANCE	Page
Making meringue	23
Lining baking sheet	45

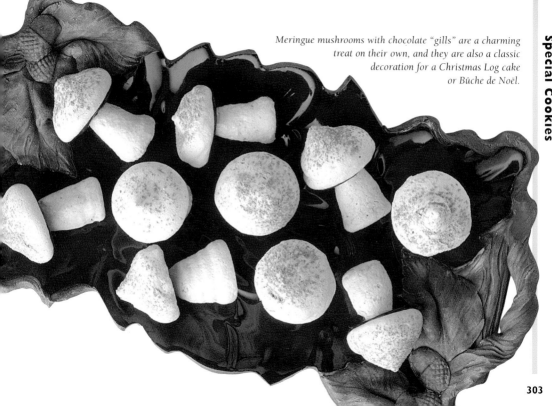

Meringue mushrooms with chocolate "gills" are a charming treat on their own, and they are also a classic decoration for a Christmas Log cake or Bûche de Noël.

METHOD FOR MAKING CHOCOLATE-DIPPED MUSHROOMS

In a medium mixing bowl let egg whites stand at room temperature for 30 minutes. Meanwhile, line 2 baking sheets with parchment paper or greaseproof paper. Set aside.

Add the vanilla and cream of tartar to egg whites. Beat with an electric mixer on medium speed till soft peaks form (tips curl). Gradually add sugar, 1 tablespoon at a time, beating on high speed till very stiff peaks form (tips stand straight) and sugar is almost dissolved. Spoon egg white mixture into a piping bag fitted with a large round nozzle (1/2-in/12-mm opening). Pipe about two-thirds of the meringue mixture into 1 1/2-in/4-cm-diameter mounds about 1 in/2.5 cm apart on prepared sheets. With remaining meringue, pipe 1-in/ 2.5-cm-tall bases about 1/2 in/ 12 mm apart on sheets.

(To get an even number of caps and stems, pipe caps and stems alternately until you've used all the meringue.)

Bake in a preheated 300°F/150°C/Gas Mark 2 oven for 20 to 25 minutes, or till meringues just begin to brown. Turn off oven. Let meringues dry in oven with the door closed for 30 minutes. Remove meringues from pans and cool on a rack.

In a small, heavy saucepan heat chocolate over low heat till melted. Spread a scant 1/2 teaspoon of the melted chocolate on the underside of each mushroom cap. Attach stems by inserting top ends in center of melted chocolate mixture, pressing gently into mushroom cap. Let mushrooms dry upside down on racks until chocolate is set.

To serve, combine icing sugar and cocoa powder. Sift over the tops of mushrooms.

Per cookie 22 calories/92 kilojoules, 0 g protein, 4 g carbohydrate, 1 g total fat (0 g saturated), 0 mg cholesterol, 3 mg sodium, 12 mg potassium

STEP 1

Piping Parts

Gently squeeze out caps and stems onto a paper-lined baking sheet using a piping bag filled with the egg white–sugar mixture. To create nicely rounded caps, hold the piping nozzle close to the baking sheet.

STEP 2

Adding Stems

Spread 1/2 teaspoon of melted chocolate on the underside of each meringue cap. Insert the pointed end of a stem into each cap, pressing slightly to secure. Dry upside down on a rack until the chocolate sets.

A triangle of tangy sour-cream dough enfolds a filling of apricot jam and white chocolate.

White Chocolate-Apricot Rugelach

These pastry-like goodies are a treat for breakfast or with morning coffee as well as after dinner. Choose your favorite flavor of jam or marmalade for the filling.

INGREDIENTS

1³/₄ cups/7 oz/220 g all-purpose (plain) flour

³/₄ cup/6 oz/185 g cold butter or margarine

¹/₂ cup/4 fl oz/125 ml sour cream

1 teaspoon vanilla extract

¹/₃ cup/4 oz/125 g apricot or raspberry jam, or orange marmalade

¹/₂ cup/3 oz/90 g white chocolate, finely chopped

2 tablespoons granulated sugar

1 teaspoon ground cinnamon (optional)

Preparation Time 45 minutes
Baking Time 20 to 25 minutes
Makes about 36 cookies

STEPS AT A GLANCE	Page
▪ Cutting in butter or margarine	84

METHOD FOR MAKING WHITE CHOCOLATE–APRICOT RUGELACH

Place flour in a mixing bowl. With a pastry blender or 2 knives, cut in butter or margarine till mixture resembles small peas. Stir in the sour cream and vanilla just till dough holds together. On a lightly floured surface, knead dough about 10 times. Divide dough into thirds. Wrap in plastic wrap.

On a lightly floured surface, roll one-third of the dough into a 10-in/25-cm circle. Spread dough with a scant 2 tablespoons of the jam or marmalade. Sprinkle with one-third of the chopped white chocolate. Cut dough into 12 wedges. Starting at curved edge, roll up each wedge. Place, point-side down, 2 in/5 cm apart on an ungreased baking sheet. Repeat with remaining dough, jam or marmalade, and white chocolate.

In a small mixing bowl stir together the sugar and, if desired, cinnamon; sprinkle over each cookie.

Bake in a preheated 375°F/190°C/Gas Mark 4 oven for 20 to 25 minutes, or till light golden brown. Remove cookies from pans and cool on a rack. Store in a tightly covered container.

Per cookie 85 calories/357 kilojoules, 1 g protein, 9 g carbohydrate, 5 g total fat (3 g saturated), 12 mg cholesterol, 49 mg sodium, 22 mg potassium

STEP 1

Cutting Dough

Roll out one-third of the dough into a 10-in/25-cm circle on a lightly floured surface and cover with fillings. With a plain or fluted pastry cutter or small chef's knife divide the dough into 12 equal wedges.

STEP 2

Shaping Cookie

Starting at the curved edge of one of the wedges, roll it toward the point, enclosing the filling. Arrange point-side down on an ungreased baking sheet. Repeat with remaining wedges. Leave 2 in/5 cm between each rolled cookie.

Glossary

Here you'll find information on selecting, purchasing, and storing ingredients used in this book.

BANANAS

Tropical bananas are usually yellow-skinned, with creamy, sweet flesh, although some varieties have red skin and pink flesh. Use slightly overripe bananas for baking. Green or unripe bananas will ripen in a few days at room temperature.

BUTTER BRITTLE PIECES

Brittle (or brickle) is a golden-brown, buttery, hard toffee. Add packaged brittle pieces to cookie doughs and batters as directed in the recipe. Available in the confectionery section of most supermarkets, these are sometimes called "toffee bits."

pumpkin

CHOCOLATE

The following chocolate types are commonly used in baking. Sweet chocolate contains at least 15 percent pure chocolate, extra cocoa butter, and sugar. Unsweetened (bitter) chocolate is pure chocolate with no sugar or flavoring, while cocoa powder is pure chocolate with very little cocoa butter. Because it lacks pure chocolate, white chocolate can't be considered a true chocolate product, although it does contain cocoa butter. Semisweet (plain) chocolate chips are interchangeable with chopped semisweet (plain) chocolate. Store well wrapped in a cool, dry place for up to 4 months.

COCONUT

The dried meat of the coconut palm adds an exotic note to cookies. It is widely available in a number of forms, including shredded and flaked, either sweetened or unsweetened. It will keep for months if stored airtight.

COFFEE

Instant coffee granules and instant espresso powder are preferred for baking because of their intense flavor and because they blend easily into batters and doughs. They will keep indefinitely if stored in an airtight container.

*semisweet (plain)
and white chocolate*

COOKING FATS

Butter, margarine, and solid vegetable shortening make cookies tender. Butter and margarine are interchangeable in almost all recipes. However, margarine made from 100 percent vegetable oil will make a very soft cookie dough that may require a longer chilling time to prevent the dough from spreading too much during baking. Use only regular margarine, not diet, whipped, or liquid forms. Shortening is a vegetable oil-based fat manufactured to stay solid at room temperature. Butter and margarine will keep for 1 month, well wrapped in the refrigerator, or up to 6 months in the freezer. Store shortening at room temperature for up to 1 year.

CREAM CHEESE

Made from a mixture of cow's cream and milk, cream cheese is appreciated for its smooth, spreadable consistency and mild, slightly tangy flavor. Available in bricks and in bulk. Refrigerate and use within a week of purchase.

DRIED FRUIT

Drying intensifies the natural flavor of fruit and concentrates its sweetness. Dried fruit, including dates, apricots, and figs, is a favorite addition to cookies. Unopened packages of dried fruit will stay wholesome almost indefinitely. Once opened, transfer to a plastic bag and store in the refrigerator.

EGGS

Cookies acquire flavor, tenderness, richness, and structure from eggs, although not every cookie recipe uses eggs. Shell color—brown or white—is purely superficial; there is no difference in quality. Refrigerate in the carton for up to 5 weeks.

FLOUR

Wheat flour gives cookies their structure. All-purpose flour has a medium protein content that makes it suitable for most baking uses. Wholemeal flour is coarsely milled from the entire wheat kernel. Store white flour in an airtight container for 10 to 15 months; store wholemeal for up to 5 months. Or, refrigerate or freeze for longer storage.

rolled oats

GINGER

The rhizome, or underground stem, of a semitropical plant, ginger is marketed fresh, dried and ground into a powder, and as candied (crystallized) pieces preserved in a syrup and coated in sugar. Select fresh ginger roots that are firm, not shrivelled. Wrap in a paper towel and refrigerate for 2 to 3 weeks. Store ground and candied ginger for up to 6 months.

JAMS AND PRESERVES

Whether sandwiched between two cookie rounds, dropped in the middle of a chewy morsel, or swirled through rich bar cookie batter, jams and preserves add color and fruity flavor to cookies of all kinds. Be sure to use the best-quality spreads you can find, with true fruit flavor that isn't masked by too much sugar.

dried fruit

LEAVENERS

Chemical leaveners give cookies a boost so they rise as they bake. Baking powder reacts with liquid and/or heat to produce bubbles of carbon dioxide that cause batters and doughs to expand. When exposed to moisture and an acidic ingredient like buttermilk, yogurt, chocolate, or lemon juice, baking soda (bicarbonate of soda) also releases carbon dioxide gas. Cream of tartar is commonly mixed with commercial baking soda and, by itself, is added to beaten egg whites as a stabilizer. Replace baking powder every 3 months.

NUTS

Almonds, hazelnuts, macadamias, peanuts, pecans, pine nuts, pistachios, and walnuts add richness, texture, and flavor to cookie doughs and fillings. You'll find them in supermarkets packaged and in bulk in a number of forms, shelled and unshelled. Store, tightly covered, in the refrigerator or freezer.

PUMPKIN

During the cool months, this winter vegetable finds its way into breads, cakes, pies, and cookies of all kinds, enhanced by spices like cinnamon, nutmeg, ginger, cloves, and allspice.

RAISINS

These dried grapes are well-loved cookie additions. Every market sells them in boxes, packages, and in bulk. Dark seedless raisins have deep color and flavor, while golden seedless (sultanas) are pale and tangy. Dark and golden raisins are interchangeable in recipes, but raisins in an ingredients list usually means the former. Store unopened packages in a dry place; once opened, seal and refrigerate or freeze.

ROLLED OATS

When oats are steamed, then flattened by steel rollers into flakes, they are sold as rolled oats or old-fashioned oats. Quick-cooking oats and rolled oats can be used interchangeably. They add bulk and flavor to cookies. Store airtight for up to 6 months or freeze for up to 1 year.

bananas

SPICES

For centuries, spices like cinnamon, cloves, allspice, nutmeg, and ginger have added their distinctive character to baked goods. All spices are available dried. Spices lose flavor after about 6 months if ground and after 2 years if whole. Store in a cool, dark, dry place.

SUGARS

These sweeteners add flavor and color to cookie doughs and batters, fillings, and frostings: dark brown sugar is a mixture of granulated sugar and molasses that adds rich, deep flavor. Light brown sugar has less molasses flavor than dark brown sugar. Confectioners sugar, also called icing sugar, is ground and mixed with a small amount of cornstarch to prevent caking. Typically, it is used for frostings and coatings. Granulated sugar is available in fine white crystals (most common) and superfine or castor (for frostings and meringues). Store sugars indefinitely in airtight containers.

*cinnamon
sticks*

SWEETENERS, LIQUID

Liquid sweeteners add their own character to cookies. Made by bees from floral nectar, honey is sweet and sticky and imparts rich flavor and perfume to batters, doughs, and fillings. Molasses is a by-product of sugar-cane refining. Light molasses is sweet and mild; dark molasses is less sweet and more full-bodied. They are interchangeable in recipes. Unopened bottles of syrup last up to a year in a cool spot; after opening, store as directed on the label. Syrup and honey will pour off more freely from a measuring spoon or cup if either is first lightly oiled.

Index

Page numbers in *italics* indicate photographs.

ACKNOWLEDGMENTS

Photography Chris Shorten, Kevin Candland, Rowan Fotheringham
Styling Susan Massey, Vicki Roberts-Russell, Laura Ferguson, Peggy Fallon